Christian organizations are both unique and complex. They operate according to priorities based on biblical principles and they demand insights and strategies far greater than those required by other profit-making organizations. Each member of the church and of other Christ-centered organizations has an important responsibility not only to use the abilities given by God but also to meet the priorities and goals set by God in the most efficient way.

Strategy for Leadership directs you toward the challenge of meeting the priorities and goals set by the Lord for your ministry. Edward Dayton and Ted Engstrom will help you discover and implement proven methods for accepting His responsibilities. This book will enable you to elevate your organization to the Lord's level of achievement.

"The two authors are recognized as authorities in the field. Their expertise should commend the book to pastors, board members, and those involved in various para-church ministries."

Bookstore Journal

"A fine aid for the pastor and/or church board chairman."

Pulpit Helps

Related books by the authors (partial listing)

THE ART OF MANAGEMENT FOR CHRISTIAN LEADERS. Ted W. Engstrom and Edward R. Dayton

THE CHRISTIAN EXECUTIVE. Ted W. Engstrom and Edward R. Dayton

THE MAKING OF A CHRISTIAN LEADER. Ted W. Engstrom

MANAGING YOUR TIME. Ted W. Engstrom and Alex MacKenzie

MISSION HANDBOOK: NORTH AMERICAN PROTESTANT MINISTRIES OVERSEAS. Edited by Edward R. Dayton

STRATEGY FOR LIVING. Edward R. Dayton and Ted W. Engstrom

TOOLS FOR TIME MANAGEMENT. Edward R. Dayton

UNREACHED PEOPLES 1979. Edward R. Dayton and C. Peter Wagner

WHAT IN THE WORLD IS GOD DOING? Ted W. Engstrom

THE WORK TRAP. Ted W. Engstrom and David J. Juroe

Strategy for Leadership

Edward R. Dayton
Ted W. Engstrom

Fleming H. Revell Company
Old Tappan, New Jersey

Library of Congress Cataloging in Publication Data

Dayton, Edward R
    Strategy for leadership.

    Bibliography: p.
    Includes index.
    1. Church management. 2. Christian leadership.
I. Engstrom, Theodore Wilhelm, 1916-   joint author.
II. Title.
BV652.D38   658′.91′25   79-11180
ISBN 0-8007-1590-X

Contents

Introduction   7

Part I   Goals, Priorities, Planning

1   Managing the Christian Organization   13
2   The Anatomy of an Organization   19
3   Christian Organizations *Are* Different   31
4   The Organizational Growth Cycle   41
5   The Awesome Power of Goals   51
6   Building on Biblical Priorities   69
7   Planning to Do God's Work   77
8   Stretching Into the Future   85
9   Problem Solving   95

Part II   Putting Basic Concepts to Work

10   Where Are You Now?   111
11   Where Do You Begin?   123
12   An Overall Approach   133
13   A Case Study   157

Part III   Methods and Tools

14   Group Planning Techniques   173
15   Planning Tools   191
16   Meetings   209
17   The Planning Conference   221

Bibliography   233
Index   236

Introduction

"What do we have to do to get this organization moving again? It feels as if we are doing the same old things and getting nowhere."

"The people of our church really want to do some new things, but we just don't seem to be able to get started. How can we get a handle on what's happening?"

"God has given us a tremendous vision of what He wants us to do! Where do we begin? How do we get started? I know the Holy Spirit's in our midst. But what tools does He want us to use?"

If you are part of a church or organization that is asking such questions, we believe that this is a book that can help you. Organizations are like people; they all have different personalities. Each one is made up of a unique mixture of individuals. The Bible calls us to see ourselves as part of a body of believers, with each part gifted in a different way, so that the total can do the work that God has called us to do. However, making this biblical model work is often frustrating for many Christians and their leaders.

Christian leaders are continually faced with the unresolvable tension between moving the work forward and caring for those doing the work. They are easily overwhelmed by being involved in activities, rather than in getting things done.

But there is a way to get things moving again. When we begin to see that an organization should be *first* thought of in terms of its purposes and goals, we can begin to focus on what it is that God has called this organization to do. The Holy Spirit can open our eyes to an entire new understanding of the organization or church of which we are a part. We can begin to see that organizations need skilled and motivated people who have adequate resources, people who are held together by an effective communication system.

The strategy for Christian leadership, then, is to help the organization restate its purpose, redefine its goals, sort out its priorities, and build God-honoring plans to move the organization forward. That is what this book is all about. We believe that—if the principles that are discussed are followed—God can use them to bring new life to your organization.

Strategy for Leadership

Part I

Goals, Priorities, Planning

1 Managing the Christian Organization
2 The Anatomy of an Organization
3 Christian Organizations *Are* Different
4 The Organizational Growth Cycle
5 The Awesome Power of Goals
6 Building on Biblical Priorities
7 Planning to Do God's Work
8 Stretching Into the Future
9 Problem Solving

1

Managing the Christian Organization

As each one has received a special gift, employ it in serving one another, as good stewards of the manifold grace of God.

1 Peter 4:10

This is a book about the management of Christian organizations. There are three key words here: *management, Christian,* and *organization.* There are many good books on the subject of management—and many different theoretical approaches to the subject. We believe that one very effective way to manage the not-for-profit organization is to zero in on the organization's goals: what it wants to accomplish, why it exists. We will advocate a four-step approach to "management for mission." It begins with goals, considers priorities, moves on to planning, and then works out those plans in the process of managing the work. This "organization growth cycle" can be pictured as a moving process that keeps repeating itself. (See Figure 1.)

Notice that we talk about management for *mission.* This is important. The Church of Jesus Christ in today's world is charged with a mission. We are to be part of His strategy. We believe that *Christian* organizations are different. We also believe that they should have a biblically based set of priorities, a Christian value system. They should ultimately see themselves in the rewarding business of bringing glory to God. Not many people recognize that a local church is undoubtedly a sophisticated organization, which demands management skills and insight that are far greater than those required for a profit-making business. Management skills may be universally useful, but Christian organizations are different.

Figure 1

We further believe that not enough is known about not-for-profit, service, and other nonbusiness types of organizations. Most of the research and writing about management and organizational theory has been concerned with profit-making organizations. Christians in general and Christian leaders in particular have given too little thought to what the Christian organization is all about. Too often there has been a nebulous idea that there is a biblical model for organizational structure which can be applied across the board. We believe strongly that there are biblical guidelines for the relationships that comprise an organization, but that every organization is in some way unique—because it is comprised of unique individuals. Most current literature deals with large organizations with staffs in the thousands. Heretofore, not enough has been written about managing the smaller organization.

Basic Concepts

In Part I we will lay down some concepts on which to build. We will attempt to dissect the organization and try to discover what an organization is and how it comes into being. We will define "Christian organization," note its special characteristics, and look at the life cycle which an organization goes through as it carries out its functions. This cycle involves goals → priorities → planning → managing.

Next we will move on to what we consider the awesome power of goals, distinguish between purposes and goals, and explain why the difference is so important. We will attempt to show how to build on biblical priorities and a Christian value system and how to plan to do God's work. We will then help you to stretch your plans into the future. In the final section of Part I we will show that getting on with the business of successful management means continually correcting toward the desired goal of problem solving.

The Concepts in Action

We will show in Part II how to put these concepts to work. This will help you establish where your organization is now and show you how to introduce the management process of goals/priorities/planning as a way of life which will lead to greater organizational effectiveness and greater glory to the One whom you serve.

Motivation will be discussed briefly. Everyone is motivated, and we need to find out what motivates people and how to attract already-motivated people by clearly announcing goals.

We will look extensively at the techniques of goals/ priorities/planning for volunteer groups and organizations. The key to effective volunteer activity is participation in the planning and goal-setting process. In this section you will also find an actual case study of how these theories have been applied.

Methods and Tools

Finally, in Part III we will introduce some tools that we think will be helpful. We will discuss group planning techniques at great length. Covered in depth will be ways of explaining plans, prioritizing goals, establishing schedules, and evaluating the results of the plans. Meetings are an important part of organizational life. We will look at how to hold effective meetings and the differences between meetings in volunteer groups and those in ongoing business organizations. This section will conclude with a chapter on holding a planning conference, a most important tool for building organizational life.

Reading Suggestions

At the end of each chapter will be found a listing of books that we believe can be of further use, those which have been particularly helpful to us. In all of this, we will offer nothing that has not been attempted and proven by others or ourselves. May God richly bless you as you get on with this beautiful business of being servants in His Kingdom.

Further Reading

For these and other reading suggestions, see bibliography for complete publishing information.

Management for the Christian Worker by Olan Hendrix is an introduction to management as a type of work needed in all Christian organizations. Illustrated by Wayne Stayskal of the *Chicago Tribune*.

The Art of Management for Christian Leaders by Ted W. Engstrom and Edward R. Dayton is a tightly packed management handbook that permits the reader to dip in at his point of need.

Managing Your Time by Ted W. Engstrom and Alex MacKenzie is written from a Christian world view. It is a general introduction to management theory, with emphasis on time management.

Sharpening the Focus of the Church by Gene Getz lays a theological framework within which to look at the church. Getz deals extensively with the roles of gifts and relationships within the organizational life of the church. (The end of the book uses a goal framework adapted from John Alexander's *Managing Our Work.*)

The Making of a Christian Leader by Ted W. Engstrom is a distillation of one Christian's thirty-five years of experience in leading Christian organizations. This book covers the whole spectrum of leadership from the biblical basis to the roles and activities of the leader.

The Effective Executive by Peter F. Drucker is one of the best. Drucker is the recognized dean of management trainers. The book is designed to help the individual to improve his insights into people and to guide others in achieving their goals while achieving one's own.

2

The Anatomy of an Organization

For just as we have many members in one body and all the members do not have the same function, so we, who are many, are one body in Christ, and individually members one of another.

Romans 12:4, 5

Has anyone ever asked you to describe your organization? If you are a pastor, you might reply, "Oh, we're Presbyterians." The mere word *Presbyterian* is supposed to give the listener an idea of how the organization works and how it is organized. If we respond with words like *Lutheran* or *Congregationalist*, we expect that our questioner will get a different picture.

If we were asked to explain why we have our kind of organization, many of us would immediately start defending it on biblical grounds. Because of our dependency upon biblical models—or because of the history of the Church—Christians tend to think of organizations as "givens." This is particularly true of the Church. We have to admit, however, that different Christian groups throughout the world have held quite opposing views of what local church organization should be.

Definitions and Origins

What is an organization? How does it come into being? How should we think about it? Let's begin at the basics and then see if we can work our way back to Christian models.

Organizations have to do with people. An "organization" occurs any time two or more people agree to carry out a task together. They may do this on the basis of some well-established precedent. Two people who agree to play tennis together are in a sense forming an organization. They have both learned the rules and have somewhat identical expectations as to what is to occur. When two people get together to cut firewood, the same type of thing occurs. Here there may be less experience on which to build, but there is a basic understanding that there is a task to perform and an assumption that the two people have an idea as to how this task is to be carried out. Moving further, two or more individuals may come together without having a clear idea of what it is they want to accomplish or how they are going to go about it. They may have nothing more than a felt need that they believe should be met. For example, they may organize a car pool for work or school. Neighbors may get together to study the Bible. A need may be within either individuals or their world.

Organizations begin with and involve people. True, we can organize machinery or other "things." But organizing humans is a different matter!

Organizations are usually bounded by time. In other words, they have a beginning and an ending in history. From the *ad hoc* organization that is formed by a pickup game of baseball to a well-established institution such as might be represented by the Roman Catholic Church, there is variation from a very short time to an indefinite period.

Organizations are formed around a purpose. Whether the purpose is despicable or lofty, unless there is an understanding of *why* the organization is formed, it is difficult for it to come into being. Another way of saying this is that organizations come into being to accomplish something. The aim may be fellowship, in which there is nothing more than the desire for mutual enhancement. Or the purpose may be a task, something that needs to be done but is outside the needs of individuals in the organization. As we will see later, the local church is in the unique situation of coming into being to accomplish both fellowship and a task.

Organizations tend to be complex—obviously, the larger the more complex. It is human relations that make them so. Every time an individual is added to an organization, the number of possible relationships grows dramatically. Consider an organization made up of two people. There is just one relationship. On the other hand, an organization made up of three people will reflect three relationships. Four people can form six potential relationships.

Carrying this further, a church with 250 members will have 31,125 possible relationships! *Note:* The formula for calculating the possible relationships (R) between a known number of people (N) is $(N^2 - N) \div 2 = R$.

Organizations come into being in the midst of a larger system. They are always related to and/or influenced by their environment or culture. This is important to note. It is very easy for us to forget that Christian organizations claim to be part of the total Body of Christ. "And the eye cannot say to the hand, 'I have no need of you . . .' " (1 Corinthians 12:21).

A Structural Hierarchy

There are many different ways of describing an organization. Most of us are familiar with organization charts and diagrams. Consider Figure 2 as an example. Here is a series of boxes and lines that are supposed to mean something. But is this a description of lines of communication within an organization? Does it show lines of authority cr responsibility? What does it really

THE ORGANIZATION AS STRUCTURAL HIERARCHY

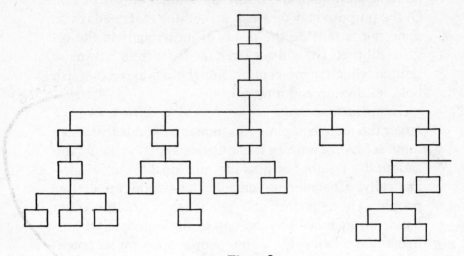

Figure 2

mean? Some of us think of organizations as hierarchical structures made up of people in different positions.

An Enabling Environment

As we have struggled to find some picture or model of an organization that might be universal to different kinds of organizations, the idea of seeing the organization as an environment appears to be useful. When we talk about our environment we mean all of the things around us. We might be concerned with the quality of the air we breathe, the school our children attend, the neighborhood we live in. When we talk about living in a poor environment, we mean that there is something there which makes our life less than it should be. When we talk about a good environment, we mean something that will make us more effective people. Thus we believe that the idea of an enabling environment is a good way to begin a description of an organization. In Figure 3 we have tried to picture such an enabling environment.

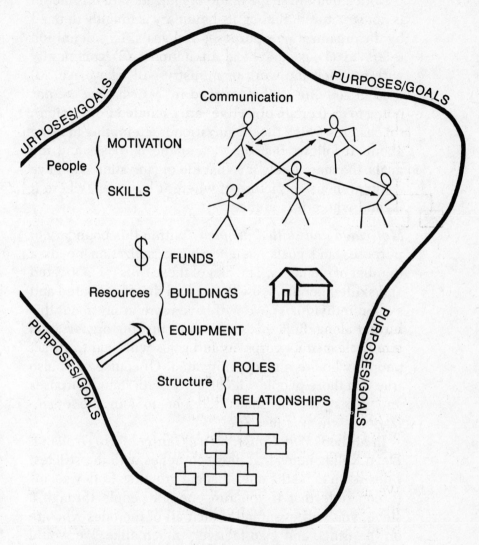

THE ORGANIZATION AS AN ENABLING ENVIRONMENT

Figure 3

Notice that the shape of the organization in this model is not structured. Rather, its boundary is roughly defined by the organization's purposes and goals. This definition refers to (1) geographical limitations; (2) community within which the work or ministry will take place; (3) kind of activities to be engaged in; (4) what we are *not* going to do (certain objectives are excluded from vision); (5) changes which the organization is attempting to bring about. It follows that the clearer the purposes and the goals, the more likely it is that the organization will have a comprehensive picture of where it has been, where it is, and where it is going.

Motivated and skilled people. Within this boundary of purposes and goals, an effective organization needs a number of elements. The first of these calls for motivated and skilled people. How do we find these motivated and skilled individuals? We will have more to say about this further along. Suffice it to say here that the organization that is clear in its purposes and goals will tend to attract people who are already motivated. Of course, it is also true that those people who disagree with stated purposes and goals will be motivated *not* to join the organization—which is just fine!

In his book *Why Conservative Churches Are Growing,* Dean Kelley notes that those churches with the strictest rules seem to be the ones that are growing. Kelley seems to conclude that if you run enough people through a sieve, you will eventually catch all of the ones who are on the fringe and who feel very much alike. We would come to a different conclusion. It would be our view that when an organization is very clear about its purposes and goals, it tends to attract people who have similar purposes and goals and to repel those who do not agree with these aims. This is why it is especially important for the local church (and any volunteer organization) to have well-stated purposes and goals. If a local church has fuzzy purposes or goals, it will find within its membership a wide and diffuse view of what the church is about. Many people will join a congregation—only to discover once "inside" that they do not agree with what they perceive to be the church's purposes and goals. Often the result is that they "go out the back door."

But a successful organization needs more than motivated members. It needs people with adequate skills. This is the dilemma of the local church, as we will see below. If the people are not skilled enough to carry out the task which has been presented to them, it really makes little difference how strongly they are motivated or how well they are led.

Adequate resources. In addition to motivated and skilled people, an organization needs adequate resources to carry out the task and to meet the personal needs of the individuals involved. These resources may be in the form of funds, buildings, equipment, facilities, and so on.

Communication. The glue that holds all of this together is good communication. It is necessary for the individuals within the organization to know what others are doing, to be able to communicate about the changes that will be taking place, and to be able to inform each other and the outside world as to where they intend to go.

Structure. Finally, there is a need for some kind of structure: a definition of the people relationships that exist and an assignment of roles. Notice that if an organization is made up of motivated, skilled people who know what the organization is trying to accomplish and how to accomplish it—and if these people are given adequate resources with which to carry out a given task, and if there exists strong communication between them—it is highly likely that they will indeed accomplish the task. In order to do this, they will go about assigning different roles within the organization. A structure will emerge. "Structure" in this sense is how we go about describing relationships. Unfortunately, such descriptions tend to be two-dimensional, and very seldom will such a description actually encompass all of the different things that make up an organization. Neglected may be such things as the responsibility of each person, the authority given to different individuals, the relationship between the various tasks, the personal relationships between individuals, and the lines of communication needed to carry out the task.

What About Your Organization?

As you think about the anatomy of your own organization, ask yourself these questions:

- Do we have clear *purposes* and *goals?*
- Are the people who make up the membership motivated towards those purposes and goals, and do they have the *skills* for accomplishing them?
- Are there adequate *resources* for us to work toward our goals? Do we have the necessary funds, energies, facilities, and buildings to do what we are trying to do with the people who are trying to do it?
- Is there a system which permits good *communication flow* between the different members of the organization? Are we so arranged that we can tell where we have been, where we are, and where we are heading?
- Is all of this put together in a *structure* which really makes this an enabling environment? In other words, does our structure really reflect our purposes and goals, the type of people on our staff, the different resources we are using, and the communication system needed to do what God wants us to do?

This is an attempt, then, to describe the organization's environment, one which we hope is enabling. But organizations are dynamic. They keep shifting and changing and moving with history. In the following section we will seek to provide another way to understand the anatomy of an organization.

A Four-Directional Tension

In Figure 4 the organization is seen as being in continuous tension as it is pulled in four directions.

HISTORY   **COMMITMENTS**

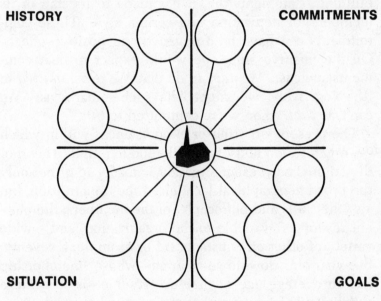

SITUATION   **GOALS**

Figure 4

The first quadrant represents *history*. Organizations are children of what has gone on in the past. How much of a task they have already accomplished will have a great influence on the present and future actions of the organization. Some organizations will have a very short view of history. Others will have a longer view. How well we remember a conversation with a friend who had recently been called to a prestigious pulpit in a major city! Knowing that his theology was somewhat more evangelical than that to which the church had been accustomed, we asked if this was causing a problem. "No," he replied. "They figure I'll be around here for no more than twenty-five years, and they can wait." This organization obviously had a long view of history, which assumed that everything would eventually turn out the way it was supposed to.

At the same time, the organization is "in tension" because of its *commitments.* Its commitments may be made up of such diverse things as the mortgage on the building, statements that it has made to its staff or its members, or dedication to a certain style. These commitments can have both negative and positive effects. On the positive side, one would expect to hear comments such as: "We *have to* do that. We're *committed* to it!" Negatively, we might hear such remarks as: "We can't do *that* when we're committed to *this.*"

The present *situation* or circumstances within which the organization finds itself will tend to pull it in another direction. The present situation is made up of not only the broad geographical location of the organization, but also the skills and philosophy of the members, the present resources available to the organization, and a wide variety of other circumstances. For example, a seventy-five-year-old downtown church—whose membership has an average age of fifty or fifty-five—is in quite a different situation from that of a relatively young suburban church which is just moving from a Christian-education building into its first sanctuary.

In tension with the quadrant of the organization's history are its *goals.* At least, there *should* be a tension here, for the organization that does not have strong goals will tend to be strung out between its present commitment and situation and pulled into its past. Goals are concepts of the future which keep the organization in creative tension. The absence or ignorance of any of these dimensions will make the organization lopsided.

From these two models (Figures 3 and 4) we can perhaps see a new way of thinking about organizations. Rather than think about them as givens, we need to see them as reflections of need, which will change dimensions with time. If we understand organizations as being defined by their purposes and goals (rather than seeing them as givens within which needs are met), we can put aside many of our traditional ideas about organizations. We are then able to move on to a new understanding of what God might have us do or be. As we relate to one another for a common purpose, we can understand what kind of organization God wants us to build.

The Plan of Study

The following chapters build on these two models of organization, which visualize the organization as being primarily defined by its purposes. If—as has been demonstrated in so many different cases—the ability of an organization to define its goals clearly and to motivate its people towards those goals is a key to organizational effectiveness, it is important to see the organization's goals as a primary concern. In the chapters that follow we will attempt more clearly to define the difference between purposes and goals. We will seek to establish some levels of priorities through which we as Christians can evaluate goals for the organization and then move into concepts of planning for the Christian organization. In all of this we will attempt to see the organization as a vehicle through which God is operating and to picture the organization as being fluid, changeable, and renewable, even as it conforms to biblical modes.

Further Reading

Organization by Ernest Dale covers all aspects of organization: line and staff, general staff, the chief executive and his staff, reorganization, international operations, and the impact of computers on organization. Many organization charts are included.

Organization Development: Its Nature, Origin and Prospects by Warren Bennis is a good introduction to emerging theories of organizational development.

3

Christian Organizations Are *Different*

*Therefore if any man is in Christ, he is a new crea-
ture; the old things passed away; behold, new things
have come.*

2 Corinthians 5:17

What is a *Christian* organization? The most obvious
Christian organization is the local church. This is the
ultimate expression of the Body of Christ in the world. It
is here that we expect to find people who are committed
to God and Christ and to God's will for themselves and
the world.

But, as we know, there is a wide variety of other Christian organizations. For example, in 1975 there were 620
Protestant agencies within the United States and Canada
whose primary emphasis was working *outside* of the
United States. We call them "missions." Within the
United States there are many types of service agencies.
These include organizations aimed at working with
youth (such as Youth for Christ and Young Life), organized groups aimed at evangelism in the United States
(such as the Billy Graham Evangelistic Association), and
those designed for particular target groups such as the
Prison Fellowship. Beyond these groups are others
which at times are more difficult to define as "Christian."
There are, for instance, publishing houses whose primary aim is to be involved in the work of Christ, even

31

though they seek to make a profit. How, then, should we define a *Christian* organization?

Definition

We believe an organization is Christian when its stated purpose is to give glory to God. Everything it does and every goal it establishes should be related to this ultimate purpose. The organization should believe that it has come into being for the purpose of establishing God's Kingdom through witnessing to the saving power of Christ, through service to others, through worship, or through building up the Body of Christ by Christian nurture.

As an aside, we might comment that we are not particularly enamored of the current term "para-church" organization. We recognize that it is useful to so describe those organizations which do not work directly through the local church or with a denomination. And yet, it has the feeling of being *outside* the Church. We recognize that there are other opinions, but we believe that the Bible teaches that each Christian, each "Christ-one" is a member of His Body, and as such is part of the total Church that He has placed in the world. In a local fellowship we find our opportunities for corporate worship and fellowship, but it may be outside this local fellowship that God has called us to additional service.

Differences

Are Christian organizations different from other kinds of organizations? We believe that they should be. There are a number of reasons why this is (or should be) so:

1. The Christian organization believes itself to be part of what God is about in the world. Or, to put it another way, we believe we are part of God's ultimate purpose. It is a legitimate goal to seek to uncover God's strategy to

the world and to become a part of it.

2. Christian organizations are made up of people who have a special relationship to one another. In many ways it is a "family corporation." This can be a problem as well as an advantage, but our experience indicates that we do well to bring into the Christian organization only those who hold a common allegiance to Jesus Christ.

3. Because of its allegiance to the Savior, the Christian organization has a set of values and priorities which are based on the Bible. This is not to say that a non-Christian or secular organization could not have the same high values. The point is that a Christian organization should assume that these values are a *given*. These values may be expressed in different behaviors. A Christian organization operating in Nairobi may express its biblical values in a different way from one operating in Chicago or Osaka. But Christians in any one of these cities should be able to identify these as *Christian* organizations. They and their members behave in a way which reflects the love, justice, mercy, righteousness, long-suffering, and patience of the biblical imperatives.

4. We have the assurance that the ultimate purpose for which we are working will one day be recognized. This is a fantastic advantage. Perhaps the power of what this means can best be demonstrated by the overseas missions of the Church. In 1975 there were 37,000 North Americans serving outside of Canada and the United States. Their total income for all operations was $650 million. If they were all in one company, that would place them well down the line on *Fortune* magazine's top 500 corporations. And yet this band of men and women has had an unbelievable impact on the world.

Assumptions About the Christian Organization

There are some basic assumptions we make as we talk about Christian organizations. These assumptions are vital to what follows. They have great implications for everything that we have to say about Christian organizations.

God has an ultimate plan for each Christian organization—be it a local church or some other expression. We hesitate to use the word *plan*, but we can think of no other word that communicates this idea. Basically, we are saying that God *is* concerned for Christians in relationship (organizations) in the same way that He is concerned for individuals. In fact, the Bible indicates that God's primary concern for individuals is in relationship to the total body of believers. But this ultimate plan, this idea that God has a future and a place for the Christian organization in His strategy, is an assumption which only the Christian organization may make.

The Holy Spirit operates through each member of the Christian organization, giving him (or her) understanding of His will. If every Christian is indwelt by the Holy Spirit who is acting to prompt the individual as to God's will for him, it follows that—within the context of the Christian organization—every member has something to say, or a word from the Lord. Again, this is both an advantage and a disadvantage. It is an advantage in that we can expect people to be motivated by a common goal, to have a common understanding of what they are trying to do. It can be a disadvantage if people assume that because they are Christians, part of the Body of Christ, their particular ideas or input should be given equal value with those of people in leadership roles.

Goals can and should be developed from within the organization. (This is a logical outcome of the second assumption.) This means that we can expect individual members to have a part in uncovering God's strategy for the organization by developing their own goals that fit into the total organization's purposes. The *purposes* of the organization may be givens and may come from without. But *goals*—stepping-stones that we use to reach our purposes—can be developed from within. We will have more to say in chapter 5 about our distinction between purposes and goals. Once again, the leadership of an organization may find this assumption at once both helpful and threatening. In organizations which are accustomed to rather authoritative styles of leadership, the idea may cause difficulty. But the concept of shared goals is a key to effectiveness for the Christian organization.

Clear and communicable goals attract clear plans. This is true for any organization, Christian or non-Christian, and is an important idea because it affects the quality of the goals with which we are dealing. When goals are well stated and thus easily communicated, they in turn will attract clear subgoals or milestones which will make up the plans of the organization. These plans express the organization's statement of faith about what it believes that God wants it to do and to become in the future.

There are many different functional forms that God may use to carry out His will. This is an assumption based upon our understanding of the Bible and the way God has worked in His Church. There are and will be different styles of leadership, management methods, and ways of organizing. There is no one "best way" for all organizations, although there is probably a best way for one particular organization at one particular time in its history. To demonstrate and substantiate this, one has only to visit the many different forms of local churches which God has seen fit to use for His glory.

We repeat, "Christian organizations *are* different." They are part of the reality of God's universe, part of God's system. It should not surprise us to discover that an understanding of Christian organizations will give us further insight into all organizations. Indeed, we believe that if we ever get real insight into how Christian organizations should operate, we will have something to say to the management of any kind of organization.

The Organizational Spectrum

Almost all Christian organizations are not-for-profit groups. We are just beginning to understand how much different from the profit-making business is the management of the not-for-profit organization, especially the volunteer organization. When someone says that the local church should be run like a business, this person does not understand how much more complicated than any business is the local church. To illustrate what we are trying to say, let us compare the breadth and degree of organizational sophistication needed by different types of organizations. Figure 5 illustrates the organizational spectrum.

At the top of this scale is the *for-profit organization,* which is narrowly defined on the one side by its market for its product or service and on the other by the need to make a profit. If the market for its services disappears, this type of organization will go out of business, as it also will if it fails to make a profit. It is true that in today's world many profit-making businesses exhibit a social responsibility. But it is just as true that if they do not make a profit or are unable to pay their employees, they will go out of business and will be unable to perform any social service. Such organizations need to have goal orientation; they need to know what product they are making or what service they are giving and where this product or service fits into the marketplace.

One step deeper in this scale of complexity is the *not-for-profit organization.* Its "market" is the need it is organized to meet. As long as it continues to meet that need, it can continue to operate. Unfortunately, the need can become quite fuzzy. The boundary indicates how well the defined need is met by the service which the

ORGANIZATIONAL SOPHISTICATION

BOUNDARY

BOUNDARY

Profit — **PROFIT ORGANIZATION** — Market

Goal oriented

Service — **NOT-FOR-PROFIT ORGANIZATION** — Need

Goal oriented

Motivation — **VOLUNTEER ORGANIZATION** — Task / Need

Goal and/or task oriented

Motivation / Personal / Limitation — **LOCAL CHURCH** — Task / Need

Fellowship oriented and task oriented

Figure 5

organization offers. If the organization is supported by freewill donations, another element is introduced, for this organization's ability to continue to operate is limited by its ability to persuade those who support it that it is indeed performing a legitimate service and meeting a real need. The not-for-profit organization is also goal oriented in that it is attempting to bring about a specific change, defined by a goal. Examples of this kind of organization would include mission agencies and some Christian service groups such as the Bible societies.

At a third level is the *volunteer organization.* This type is much more difficult to comprehend and to manage because it is highly dependent upon its ability to motivate its members to service. Its ability to recruit and motivate is becoming increasingly more difficult in a society where there are more and more choices, more and more places where the volunteer can serve. A quick look at the Yellow Pages of any phone book will indicate a surprisingly large number of volunteer organizations in towns of every size. Thus, the boundary on the one side is its ability to motivate people to service. Christian organizations using large numbers of volunteers to carry out their work would include Child Evangelism Fellowship (which uses volunteers to conduct home Bible classes), the Gideons (which uses volunteers to distribute Bibles), and branches of the local church (such as the Sunday school). Note that in all of these examples there is the assumption that those volunteers will be expected to be capable of carrying out their assignments.

On the other side, the volunteer organization is bounded by both need and the task that it is seeking to carry out. For example, it may be operating a "help line" emergency telephone. Here the goal is difficult to define. It is a service, described by the task that is being carried out: dealing with people's needs over the telephone.

At the greatest depth and breadth of our scale is the most sophisticated and the most difficult organization to manage—the *local church*. Why? Because the local church seeks at one time to care for its members while at the same time using them for its task. And to do this it must accept all those who volunteer. The only qualification for joining this organization is to be "a friend of the Boss"! In other words, if you accept Jesus as Lord and Savior and are willing to abide by whatever rules the local church has established, by definition you are accepted as a member. It doesn't make any difference whether the organization has a specific place or function for you to perform. You are accepted.

This organization, by definition, accepts the "walking wounded" along with the skilled and unskilled. Imagine how you would feel if one day there were a knock at the door of the business you were managing. Outside are four men carrying another on a stretcher. Their friend is deaf and dumb and physically incapacitated but "loves the Lord and wants to be a member of your organization." What would you do with such a person? He doesn't fit any job description that you have anywhere. The manager of any organization with the sole purpose of accomplishing a task could only say, "Sorry!" and send the person away. Yet that is the dilemma faced by the pastor (manager) of the local church.

So this organization, the local church, is bounded on the one hand by both task and need. On the other hand, the church is bounded by its ability to motivate people and by their personal limitations. In addition to being goal oriented, the organization must be fellowship oriented at the same time.

Irreconcilable Goals?

Here we have the crux of the organizational difficulty of the local church. For the local church has two irreconcilable and simultaneous goals: (1) to care for its members; (2) to send these people forth in acts of service for Christ. It can neither put up a NO HELP WANTED sign, nor decide that the task must take precedence over the nurture of its members. And yet it cannot decide that the individual member is more important than the task of the church!

This is the reason the key to effective ministry and management for the local church is through clear purposes and well-stated goals. Indeed, most of the "church growth" literature from around the world indicates that the one common denominator is the idea of having a goal or a desire to grow. Over and over we will emphasize the need to enter into the management problems of church organization through the doorway of purposes and goals.

Further Reading

Sharpening the Focus of the Church by Gene Getz. (See reading list for chapter 1.)

Competent to Lead by Kenneth Gangel is a serious attempt at biblical theological management.

4

The Organizational Growth Cycle

But they that wait upon the Lord shall renew their strength; they shall mount up with wings as eagles; they shall run, and not be weary; and they shall walk, and not faint.

Isaiah 40:31 KJV

Organizations, like individuals, tend to have growth cycles. In Figure 6 we have shown a typical organizational cycle from the viewpoint of the leader.

This cycle begins when an individual (or a group of people) gathers others around a common purpose or goal. The individual or group decides that there is a need to be met.

The Cycle in Action

For example, we may see that there is a real need for a ministry to senior citizens within our community. We may uncover the fact that many senior citizens are isolated in homes for the aged where there is little spiritual nurture and minimal emotional support.

Purpose and goal setting. At this point we may only have a very generalized *purpose:* "Something should be done for those people." There are many things that we might be able to do. Which ones should we do? Which ones are God's best goals for us? If we already have some other ministries, where does this new ministry fit in relation to the others? Specifically what is it that we want to see done? This is *goal setting.*

41

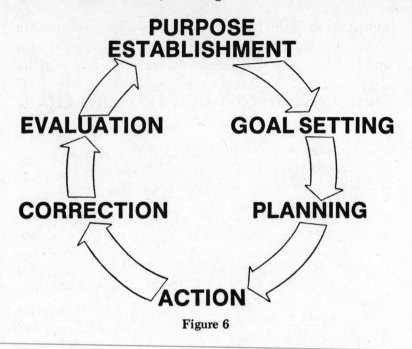

Figure 6

Planning.   Having established what it is we want to accomplish, we then set about figuring how we might accomplish our goals. We go about the business of planning. This is usually carried out on an intellectual level without any apparent action on our part. True, many people may just start acting without doing any planning. But in reality they are planning (or correcting) as they act. However, in almost every case we go through some mental exercise of deciding how we will reach the goals, choosing between different alternatives, and deciding on means and methods. If, for example, we have decided that we would like to have daily telephone contact with all the individuals in a particular retirement home, we have much to decide. How many calls will we have to make? How many callers will we need? What will we have to do in terms of getting permission from the administration of the home? How will we motivate people to become callers? How will we handle the questions and problems that will naturally arise in the course of the conversations? What other ministries may this lead to? All of these different components need to be fitted together in some kind of plan.

Action.   The next step for the leadership is to manage subsequent events, to begin to take *action*. There may be a number of things that we need to do before we can actually set about reaching toward the goal. For instance, we may have to gather some resources together. To continue our illustration of a senior-citizen ministry, we might need access to telephones, or have to publish a letter—anything that is needed to carry out the action. We then begin to act specifically. There may be a series of actions: contacting the owners of the senior citizens' home, making arrangements for the timing of the calls, recruiting people, holding training meetings—a wide variety of things which may be described as "acting." In management parlance this might be called "organizing," but it is seldom thought of in this way by new organizations. To put it another way, the individuals involved have little self-awareness as an organization, at this point. But an organization has come into being just by the fact that a number of individuals have agreed to accomplish a particular goal.

Correction.   In the midst of managing action there will come a need for *correction*. Things seldom turn out the way we have imagined them. Someone has said that the chances of something going wrong far outnumber the chances of things going right! Therefore, we need to recognize that where plans and/or actions are not helping us to achieve our goals, we must make new plans or change our actions. In practice, this correcting goes on all of the time. We may discover that we hadn't planned on enough telephone callers or that the conversations were taking longer than we expected. Perhaps the cooperation that was promised by the administration of the senior citizens' home does not materialize, or there was a misunderstanding. This is what "management" is all about.

Evaluation.   Before the organization can move on toward reacting and enlarging its growth cycle by modifying its purposes and its goals, it must undergo *evaluation* of the entire process, to see whether the initial purposes and goals have been met. This process of evaluation is probably the most important step in the life and growth of any organization. As we shall see, a failure here can have major consequences down the road. For example, we may discover that we are causing more distress among the older people in these homes than we expected. Perhaps the telephone calls weren't a very good idea. Possibly it would have been much better if we called in person or set up a weekly meeting.

A Repetitive Process

We have purposely shown this process as a circle or cycle, a recurring or repetitive process. In the ideal situation, the organization begins with purposes; goes through the cycle to discover better purposes, set more effective goals, establish clearer priorities, do better planning, do a better job of managing; and then goes on with the reevaluation.

Note, too, that this model takes into account both the short and the long-range lives of the organization. It pictures what happens to the total organization as well as to one particular part of the organization. As a short-range example, suppose that you are responsible for re-

cruiting telephone callers. Your goal is to have six telephone callers available between nine and twelve o'clock
every day. You have to decide where this goal fits into
the priorities of all the other goals that you have to carry
out and then allow enough time for it. It is necessary to
make specific plans about how you are going to find the
right people, how many people you are going to need (to
produce six each day), and what kind of instructions you
are going to have to give them. Then, after you have
recruited them, you need to manage the program by
making sure that they are actually there each day, that
back-up people are available, and that their questions
are answered. As a result of this, you may want to modify
your goal—for example, by having eight people on call
rather than six.

In the larger, long-range picture, this growth cycle
may lead to a city-wide organization with the primary
purpose of meeting all the needs of the senior citizens
within that particular city.

Overlapping Functions

Figure 6 fails to take into account that a number of
these steps or functions may overlap or be interrelated.
In Figure 7 we indicate that purposes and goals establish
direction—as part of our evaluation of history or what has
gone on in the past. For example, in our illustration of
the senior citizens' ministry, when the initial purposes of
the new organization were established, they were based
upon an evaluation of what others had done (events that
had led up to this moment). Therefore, the process of
setting *goals* based on *purposes* is very much wrapped
up with the *evaluation* process.

At the same time, *planning* and *correcting* encompass
acting. When we talk about taking a corrective action,
we are talking about doing some planning, making new

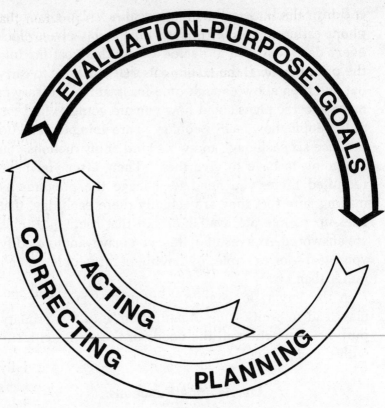

Figure 7

plans which will reflect the situation as we now see it.

This rather simple diagram fails to describe the "wheels within wheels" that make up most organizations. If an organization is carrying out a number of different ministries, each of these ministries may be in a different place at a different time. For example, in the local church we may (1) be trying to establish some goals for our Christian education program next year; (2) be trying to sort out our priorities among the priorities we have previously discussed for our evangelism program eight months hence; (3) be right in the midst of planning leaders for next year's home Bible study; (4) be very much in the midst of a summer outreach program that keeps presenting us with new "challenges" each day.

Why Organizations Fail or Falter

This repetitive process which we have shown in Figures 6 and 7 helps us to understand why organizations fail or falter. Essentially an organization fails when it does not achieve its purpose. This may be the result of unrealistic goals. It may be that goals were set too high—or, on the other hand, they may have been set too low. They may have been inadequate to reach the purposes.

We may not have spent enough time on our priorities. There may have been *too many* good things to do. We never sorted out which one was most important and consequently dissipated our energies and our resources by trying to do too many things at once. For example, trying to have church services in a senior citizens' home, organizing an escort service for them, setting up a daily telephone check, and supplying financial-aid programs may have all been very worthwhile goals—but the new organization would have difficulty doing them all at once.

A third point of failure in the process may be that the planning was inadequate or limited. If we have not taken into account enough of the possible alternatives, we may not have been able to meet the circumstances that came about as a result of the actions of the organization. It is probably at this point that more organizations fail to get off the ground than any other. It is not sufficient to consider only what it is that we would like to happen. We must follow through and try to think about the consequences of our action.

Moving on to the next step, there may be failure because of our inability to follow the plans that we have made or to see the necessity for changing plans. We may fall into the trap of believing that we should doggedly follow an initial plan. In other words, our plan was controlling us rather than the other way around. In The Living Bible paraphrase of Proverbs 13:19, we read: "It is pleasant to see plans develop. That is why fools refuse to give them up even when they are wrong."

Another reason for failure may be an absence of adequate resources to carry out our plans. Jesus warns us about counting the cost before starting to build. Most Christian work is based on the assumption that God will provide the funds through those who will be moved by His Spirit to support the work. Somewhere there needs to be a balance between our desire to see something happen and our faithful belief that there will be those who will support what we are about.

As we close the circle, a failure can occur because we do not reassess or review our purposes and have not learned the lessons of history. We assume that what we set out to do is correct and that there is no need to modify it. This is a real tension. We need to be single-minded in our purposes, and yet too often this becomes narrow-mindedness and we fail to see all that God may be trying to show us.

Finally, an organization can fail because the action that is taken becomes an end in itself. The function becomes the purpose. The organization becomes wrapped up in what it is doing, rather than in what it is *achieving*. An organization may have been successfully through the cycle a number of times and still fail. As organizations become more "efficient," they may become less effective. Instead of designing new plans for new situations, there may be an assumption that the old plans ("the way we have always done it") are still the way to go.

Surprisingly, a major reason for failure can be success! Many times an organization which was successful in achieving its initial purpose comes to believe that it has done everything right and that the way it has done things in the past will therefore be exactly the way to do things in the future. But times do change, and it is vitally important that organizations change with them.

The Healthy Organization

Organizations need to stay in orbit. As long as they continue to move through the steps of goals, priorities, planning, and managing—followed repeatedly by the same process—they will tend to stay healthy and grow. Now that we have sought to describe an organizational growth cycle, we will dig deeper and take a look at each one of these major steps.

Further Reading

Organization by Ernest Dale. (See reading list for chapter 2.)

Organization Development by Warren Bennis. (See reading list for chapter 2.)

5

The Awesome Power of Goals

. . . forgetting what lies behind and reaching forward to what lies ahead, I press on toward the goal for the prize of the upward call of God in Christ Jesus.

Philippians 3:13, 14

There are few things more powerful than the idea of a goal, as Paul reminds us. All through the ages, the imagination of men and women has been captured by the idea of a goal, the dream of what might be, what God might desire.

Up until this point we have been using the words *purpose* and *goal* rather interchangeably. Before moving further, we need to come to more specific terms. It is not as important that you agree with our definitions as it is that you understand what we mean. *What we are about to discuss can do more to change the future of your organization than anything else that we will say in this book.*

Too often, Christians spend time arguing about the meaning of words rather than attemping to understand one another. This is quite natural when one considers how important words are to us. After all, we are people of The Book. We assume that we have a revelation that has been given to us, an inspired Word from God. Therefore, the words *justification, salvation, sanctification,* and so on have a great deal of importance to us. We are disturbed when people take words that we believe mean one thing and pour a different content into them. But when we use words that are part of the everyday coinage of living, it is less important that we agree on the exact meaning of the word than it is that we understand what the other person means when he uses that word. We need to have fellowship around the facts.

This is why it is important that we clearly distinguish between what we will call a "purpose" and a "goal." You may have different definitions for these words, but try to understand what we mean by them. Where we use the word *purpose,* you may be used to thinking about an "aim," a "mandate," or perhaps a "mission." Perhaps you are used to calling "goal" what we define as a "purpose." On the other hand, where we use the word *goal,* you may be used to calling such a concept an "objective," a "milestone," or a "task." These words are used in different ways by different people in different kinds of organizations. We purposely limit ourselves to the two words *purpose* and *goal.* For us, the basic distinction between the two pertains to our ability to measure.

What Is a Purpose?

A purpose is something for which we ultimately hope. It is not necessarily measurable in itself, but it is a clear direction toward which we wish to move. "To give glory to God" is a purpose. "To have a God-honoring church" is a purpose. "To be a good Christian" is a purpose. These are all very desirable. No one would argue that they are not something towards which we should move.

We need purposes. They set directions for our individual and corporate lives. But we also need to put some content into these purposes, to state what we think is likely to happen if we move in a given direction—what the outcomes will be. Unfortunately, Christian organizations have a great tendency to define their purposes and never get around to stating clearly what they intend to *do.* They suffer from "fuzzability thinking." They state things in such broad terms that it is often difficult to tell whether they have accomplished what they set out to do.

Take the case of a youth meeting that is being planned. The scheduled church hall could hold well over a hundred people. There are about sixty in the youth group normally. The youth leaders have the purpose of "having an inspiring and exciting evening," but that's as far as they have gone in their thinking. Different people have been given assignments for leading a Bible study, designing games, or bringing the refreshments. In the back of the leader's mind is the idea that there will be about fifty or sixty people at the meeting, which is scheduled for eight o'clock. By eight-thirty it is obvious that there are not going to be more than thirty-five young people present. The next day the pastor may ask the youth leader, "How did it go last night?"—and "Well, the Lord was really present!" may be the reply.

That *is* true. The Lord really was present. But what happened? Sixty young people were expected (there was room for more), and only about half showed up. We effectively "spiritualize" away our intentions so that it won't appear that we have failed.

This leads us quite naturally to the need to come up with some *definable* and *measurable* statements of purpose. We call these "goals."

What Is a Goal?

A goal, by our definition, is first an image or a picture of the future. We are not very much concerned with setting goals for the organization of two months ago! Goals are future events. Therefore, for the Christian organization, a goal—this picture of the future—*is a statement of faith.* Don't miss that one! We need to recognize this when we begin to be concerned about "failure."

The next quality of a goal is that we believe it can be

accomplished. The people who set the goal believe that it is practical, or at least possible. They have a clear picture of what the world will be like when this future event is accomplished.

Another characteristic of a goal—over and against a purpose—is that it can be measured in two ways. It is here that our definition clearly differentiates between goals and purposes. First, a goal can be measured by *time*. We will know the date by which it will be accomplished or when it will be put into effect. We also should be able to measure it by *performance*. We will be able to establish the fact that the goal has been reached, the event has happened. In other words, it will become a past event.

In his delightful book *Goal Analysis*, Robert Mager presents us with the "Hey, Dad, watch me" test. If you want to find out whether you have a real goal (one which can be measured by time and performance), put that phrase in front of the goal statement. You might say, "I want to become a self-actualized person." Is that a goal? If we try it with the test—"Hey, Dad, watch me *become a self-actualized person!*"—we find that we don't really know what is going to be *done*. Dad may say, "Okay, son, go ahead!"—but how will he know that you have become a "self-actualized person"?

Another way of saying all this is that *a goal is a future event towards which we can measure progress*. Although a goal may change or be modified by future circumstances, as best we know at a point in time, it is what we believe we should accomplish. It is important to see that goals are not ends in themselves, but merely steps along the way in the life of the organization. Just as purposes without goals can be discouraging, goals without purposes can be hopeless. There must be some ultimate purpose towards which the Christian organization is moving.

Why Are We Afraid of Goals?

Why is it that many Christian organizations never get around to expressing their goals—stating those future events that they hope will occur as a result of their service before the Lord? There are a number of reasons, but two appear to be paramount:

Fear of failure. Many times we are afraid of failure. After all, if we say that we will do such-and-such a thing by such-and-such a time, and it does not come about, we will feel that we have "failed." A number of things can be said at this point. The first observation has already been made: Life seems to be full of many more chances for failure than for success. It is rather interesting to note that when a major-league ball player goes to bat, he fails more times than he succeeds. Indeed, the individual who hits three times out of ten (bats .300) is considered to be quite a success!

But perhaps we are afraid to fail because we have taken upon ourselves too much responsibility for the task we are about. Remember that this is supposed to be God's business! If goals are statements of faith, we expect that God is going to honor our faith by using what we have done for His glory. Think of it this way: When we set goals for the organization, we are essentially saying, "Lord, here is our understanding of what You would have us to do. This is our statement about the way we think the world should be in the future, based on our belief about what would be pleasing to You. Where we are wrong, give us insight. Where we are right, strengthen our hand."

God's sovereignty vs. man's responsibility. Another major reason we fear goals is that we are afraid that people may think we are trying to "do the work of the Holy Spirit." They picture any attempt to describe the future as trying to take over what they consider to be

God's domain. We realize that there is an age-old theological tension here between the sovereignty of God and the responsibility of man. In our view we do well to accept the biblical paradox that although God is completely in charge, we are totally responsible for the world. Of course, we are doing the work of the Holy Spirit! If that is not what we are about, then we are not involved in a *Christian* organization!

The Power of Goals

1. Goals give a sense of direction and purpose. They tell workers where the organization is going and help them to see where they fit. "If you don't know where you're going, any road will take you there." Perhaps it is better said in the words of the Prophet Amos: "Can two walk together, except they be agreed?" (Amos 3:3 KJV).

2. Goals give us the power to live in the present. We can't really make any decisions about the future. We are not even sure who will be alive at any given time in the future. But if we know the kind of desirable future that we want, we can make decisions *today* which are more likely to bring us into that future. Goals—statements of faith about the future—help us to do that.

3. Goals promote enthusiasm and strong organizational life. When people know that they are working together for the common good, there is an increased sense of fellowship. It is much easier to build fellowship around a task that people are accomplishing together than it is to build fellowship for fellowship's sake. How many times have you had the experience of trying to get together to "have fellowship," only to discover that there was little to have fellowship about? On the other hand, remember the excitement of accomplishing a common goal with other people!

4. Goals help us to operate more effectively. They don't necessarily help us to operate more *efficiently*, since we may change our goals and therefore have to change the way we work. But they do emphasize *effectiveness*. One definition of a problem is "a deviation from a goal." The assumption is that if there is no goal from which to deviate, we really don't have a problem. Goals tell us where to put our energies.

5. Goals help us to evaluate our progress. This also increases our effectiveness. If we don't know how far we have come, how can we know whether we have arrived?

6. Goals force us to plan ahead. They help us to look at the future and not focus our attention on the past. Remember our model of an organization pulled in four different directions by its history, situation, commitments, and goals?

7. Goals help us to communicate within the organization. They tell us where we are going and how we are doing. Have you ever said to yourself, "I wonder who's responsible for *that!*"? Evidently you didn't have a clear picture of who had the assigned responsibility for that particular goal. This is why it's important that different departments and sections be organized around goals rather than around tasks.

8. Goals give people a clear understanding of what is expected. This helps the individual to see how he or she is doing. This is the whole concept behind "management by objectives" (MBO). The exciting thing about having a goal is seeing ourselves moving toward it. If the members of an organization are not given specific goals, they have no way of knowing whether or not they are being "successful."

9. Goals help to reduce needless conflict and duplication of effort. Too often, when goals are unclear, two people may be doing the same thing without knowing it. We have also all run into the response of "Oh, I thought that was *your* responsibility!" Goals therefore reduce the needless misunderstanding which results from having unclear aims.

10. Goals take the emphasis off activity and place it on output. It is not how much we do (activity) that counts, but what we get done (output). The organization which focuses on all the good things it does, rather than on the goals it accomplishes, is on the road to failure.

Goal Relationships

In any organization there is (or should be) a relationship between all of the goals. There are a number of different kinds of relationships, but the two most important are (1) the dependency of some goals upon others; and (2) the relationship of goals to one another in time.

In Figure 8 we have shown a series of goals represented by boxes. The arrows are intended to show that in order to accomplish the highest goal—our *primary* goal—it is necessary to achieve the three goals below it—our *secondary* goals. You have seen situations like this many times. Suppose, for example, you wanted to begin a special series of programs by June 1, perhaps a group of evangelistic meetings. To meet the goal of "beginning," there are a number of things which must be done. Someone has to have a goal of having the facility prepared. Someone else has to have a goal of having the various participants briefed. Still another may have a goal of making sure that people are invited. These three goals all have to be met before the higher goal of being ready to start is accomplished. These lower goals will be supported by other goals that might have to do with the everyday things of life—such things as making sure that the buildings are heated, that the weekly communica-

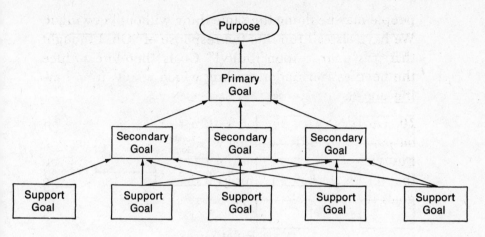

GOAL DEPENDENCIES

Figure 8

tion bulletin is issued, that the needs of the staff are met, and so on.

What names or titles are given to the different goal levels are not important. Some people might call the goal at the top a "primary" goal and the ones underneath the "secondary" goals. Others might wish to use such terms as "subgoals," "milestones," or "objectives." The important thing is to see the relationships. Whatever terms you use to describe your goals, make sure that everyone is using the same language.

We have already indicated that a number of different people may be the "goal owners." One person's primary goal may be another person's secondary goal. If I am the person ultimately responsible for the primary goal of starting the program, I may view the goal of "having the facility ready" as a secondary goal. If, on the other hand, I am the person responsible for that facility goal, this will be *my* primary goal. Thus we see that goals help people relate to one another. It is important that I understand what *your* goals are, so that I can see how *my* goals relate

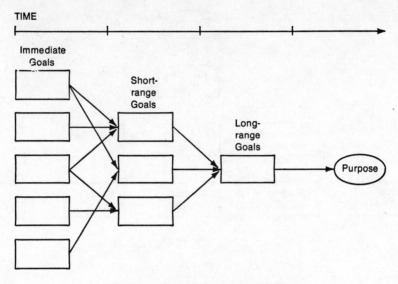

GOALS AND TIME DEPENDENCIES

Figure 9

to yours. Strong organizational life is built upon such an understanding.

The second relationship that goals have to one another is contingent on time. In Figure 9 we have shown the same diagram as in Figure 8—this time turned on its side, with the time direction from left to right. The goals at the extreme left might be called immediate goals, things that have to be done right now. The ones in the middle might be called short-range goals, while the ultimate goals might be the long-range ones.

Note that these are relative terms. The long-range goal of one activity may be different from the long-range goal of another activity. For instance, the long-range goal of a baseball game is to win the ball game, perhaps two or three hours from now. The long-range ten-year goal of the space program was to get a man on the moon and return him safely.

So we see that goals are not only related to one another

but are related in time. The goals of an organization impact upon one another in the same way as do the events of history. It turns out that plans are nothing more than a series of goals. When we talk about taking steps toward a goal, we are really talking about a subgoal (a step) which really moves us toward another goal. When we note that we had better do "this" thing before we do "that" thing, we are recognizing that one goal is time-dependent upon another.

Clear Goals vs. Fuzzy Goals

Sometimes we have difficulty stating goals that accurately communicate what we want to do. The two relationships that we have just discussed—dependency and time—can help us here. If you are having difficulty stating a goal, attempt to state what things must happen before the goal is reached—or attempt to state first the general purpose and then what goals are needed to make this purpose a reality. For example, suppose that about the best you can say of a Christian education program is that you "would like to have adults know more about the Bible." What are some of the things that might have to happen before adults have better knowledge of the Bible? Here are some goals that might support such a general "fuzzy" idea:

1. Twenty-five adults will complete a ten-week survey course of the Bible by June 30.
2. Four Sunday evenings will be given over to one hour of Bible expositions during the month of May.
3. A new translation of the Bible will be placed in the pew racks in the church—with one Bible for every two people by June 22.

You can't *prove* that any of these goals will actually give adults better knowledge of the Bible. They are your statements of faith about what you believe you should do in order to see this accomplished.

This leads us to the questions of stating or writing goals accurately. Well-written goals are:

1. Stated in terms of end results, as past events.
2. Achievable in a definite time. We know when they will become past events.
3. Definite as to what is expected.
4. Practical and feasible. We believe we know how to reach them.
5. Precisely stated in terms of quantities, where possible.
6. Limited to one important goal per statement.

Poorly written goals tend to be:

1. Stated in terms of process or activity. They emphasize *doing* things.
2. Never fully achievable, no specific target dates set.
3. Ambiguous as to what is expected.
4. Theoretical or idealistic.
5. Too brief and indefinite, or too long and complex.
6. Written with two or more goals per statement.

Goal Setting As a Process

It is very easy to think that once we have clearly stated our goals, our job is done. We imagine that now all we need to do is to get on with the business of reaching our goals. One tends to believe that if one just really knew what the future should be like, one could press on towards it without turning to the left or to the right. But the future that lies before us will be quite different from the future we expect. Change will come—individually and organizationally. Others will change; the needs of the world will change; situations will change. This means that the review and reestablishment of our goals is a process which must go on continually. That is why we show "management for mission" as a cycle, and why we say that goals point direction, rather than define precisely where we will eventually arrive.

Operational Goals

It is one thing to write down or state a goal. It is quite another to carry it out. Because organizations are comprised of many individuals, the possibility for failure is increased as the number of relationships increases. When an individual has a personal goal, he can often be the goal setter, planner, and executor all wrapped up in one. If he changes his mind, he knows exactly to whom to give instructions—himself. But organizations are dependent upon individuals' working together. Before a goal can become operational and put into effect, it must have some additional characteristics.

1. A goal should be related in some way to the organization's purposes.

2. We must believe we can do it. Goals are often set so high that they are unrealistic. People are not really convinced that the organization can accomplish the goal. In fact, they may believe it is just a dream put up there as a "target" by the leadership. For example, suppose a growth-minded pastor challenges each member of his congregation to bring five new people "next Sunday." That 2 or 3 percent of the people might be able to do this is believable, but not that all of the congregation will be able to do it—particularly when the church could seat only one-quarter of them if they all came. This goal is unrealistic and thus fails to challenge. On the other hand, if the goal were for each to bring *one*, that would be believable.

3. A goal should have a date when it will be accomplished. We should know when we want it done. It ultimately should be in the past tense. If people do not have a clear picture as to the time frame within which a goal lies, they have entirely different assumptions as to how urgent it is. "Let's get in there and double our giving!" doesn't mean very much until someone says *when* (and, of course, *how*).

4. A goal must be measurable.   Everyone must be able to tell that it has happened, that it has become a past event. If we don't make goals measurable, we will take away from people their sense of accomplishment. If the goal is "double the giving," we had better decide how much money this will produce.

5. A goal needs to be supported by a plan.   The point here is that we must know *how* we plan to reach the goal. We must believe we can get "there" from "here," and have some understanding of which way the path will lead.

6. A goal needs to be claimed by someone.   Someone must believe that he owns it. We must all know *who* will take the steps to reach the goal. What is everyone's business is *no one's* business. The question is not whether we all believe in the goal, but who believes in it enough to make it happen.

7. A goal must be supported by the necessary resources. We must have an understanding of what it is going to cost in money, facilities, and other types of "energy," and we must have these resources available. Too often, Christian organizations begin with money when they should begin with goals. But the fact remains that if the people do not have the energy to carry it off, the goal will not become operational.

These characteristics of an operational goal are shown in worksheet form in Figure 10. You may want to make a copy of this and use it with groups in your own organization. It may be too short for many goals. On the other hand, it has the ability to communicate what we are saying here. If you present this form without going through all the explanations, you may be able to communicate the concepts by doing, rather than explaining (a much better way to learn).

Guidelines for Goal Setting

Limit goals to major objectives. These should be accomplished during a given time. In other words. don't clutter up the future with goals that are so far in the future that they don't seem real to the participants.

Assign goals to people and then hold them accountable for them. At the same time, allow room for flexibility and change. Things will be different from what we expected. There may be legitimate reasons for modifying a goal as we go along. The important thing here is to make sure that such a goal *is* restated in different terms, rather than just abandoned.

Keep the goal-setting process simple and flexible. Avoid too many rigid forms, overdocumentation, and things which tend to confuse people. Remember, *you* may understand the process, but it is not going to work unless the people who have to put it into operation understand it.

Take people into account in setting and assigning organizational goals. Some goals will have to be tailored to the gifts, skills, and potential contribution of an individual. Too often we set up idealized goals which demand such an outstanding person that they become just that—unattainable ideals.

Provide guidance in helping individuals set realistic goals for themselves. If allowed to set their own goals, most people will set them too high. This is good, but it can be discouraging if the people consistently fail to reach their own goals.

Don't set goals in a vacuum. Get people involved. It

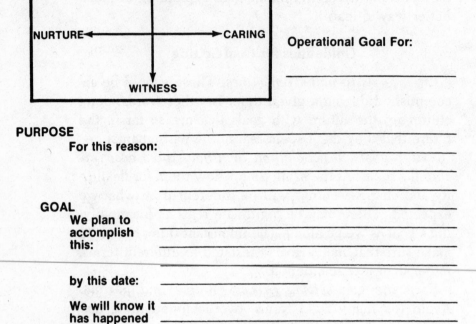

WORSHIP

NURTURE ← → CARING

WITNESS

Operational Goal For:

_____

PURPOSE
     For this reason: _____
_____
_____
_____

GOAL
     We plan to
     accomplish
     this: _____
_____
_____
_____

     by this date: _____

     We will know it
     has happened
     because: _____

STEPS
     We plan to
     take these
     steps: _____
_____
_____
_____

PEOPLE
     These people
     are responsible: _____

COST
     It will cost
     this amount: _____

Figure 10

may seem trite, but good goals are *our* goals and bad goals are *their* goals.

Final Assumptions About Goals

As we conclude this chapter on goals and goal setting, it might be useful to state some additional assumptions . . . .

Goal setting assumes that *people are more willing to commit themselves to goals which they participated in setting* and are less likely to commit themselves to goals that originated with others. We are much more likely to want to work on something that has been our own idea.

Goal setting assumes that *people perform better if they can measure their progress.* If I know where I am going and can see how I am doing, I can see whether I have to work harder and more carefully, or perhaps even slow down.

Goal setting assumes that *most people desire to make a significant contribution* to the organization if they are given the opportunity. Time and time again this has proven so in practice.

Goal setting *utilizes the concept of delegation and mutual agreement* on what has been delegated. By announcing that "this is *your* goal," we are in a sense telling a person that he is responsible, and he can know clearly where the limits of the delegation lie.

Goal setting *emphasizes results rather than means.* This cannot be overemphasized.

Goal setting assumes that *people perform better when they have some control over their future.* Goals (statements of faith) help us to define together what we think the future should be like, and therefore help us to relax in these statements of faith, trusting in God's good will for us.

Good goals and bad goals.   One final word about goals. Good goals are *our* goals and bad goals are *their* goals. The goals we appreciate most and to which we are committed are *our* goals, those which we have shared in defining.

Further Reading

God's Purpose and Man's Plans by Edward R. Dayton is a workbook particularly aimed at the manager involved in Christian organizations. It has two programmed instructions to motivate people toward goal setting—plus two sections: one on planning and one on problem solving.

Goal Analysis by Robert F. Mager is a delightful book with some programmed instruction that will really help people understand the differences between real goals and fuzzy goals. Mager's "Hey, Dad, Watch Me" Test is a simple but excellent way to discover whether one really has a goal.

Goal Setting: Key to Organizational Effectiveness by Charles L. Hughes is a McKinsey Award book which describes how overall objectives can be broken down into subgoals for managers and employees at all levels.

Goal Setting: A Guide to Achieving the Church's Mission by Dale D. McKonkey is an exceptionally good small guide that local churches should find very useful. It is written in churchly language, is extremely clear, short, and to the point (32 pages). This is part of the Administration Series for Churches.

6

Building on Biblical Priorities

And He gave some as apostles, and some as prophets, and some as evangelists, and some as pastors and teachers, for the equipping of the saints for the work of service, to the building up of the body of Christ.
Ephesians 4:11, 12

What is a priority? Some will respond in terms of putting one thing before something else. Others may think in terms of ranking items. Priorities have both a "when" and an "if."

There are many priority questions. For the Christian organization there is the question of which purpose—of all the possible ministries with which we could become involved—is the one that God wants for *our* organization? Once we become involved in a ministry, we face the question of a choice between goals. Thus, of all the things that we could do to carry out the ministry, which seem most important to us now? Which should be postponed? Which should be abandoned? We can also think of priorities in terms of allegiance. What claims the highest priority in our lives?

Levels of Christian Priority

Christian organizations are comprised of the people of God in relationship. Although other organizations may claim to represent relationships, the Christian organization represents a special association, since each of its members is part of a larger family, the Body of Christ.

In addition, the organization itself claims to be part of this larger body of believers—the Church—which is both mystical and physical. The Bible indicates that the work of Christ is to be done by people in relationship, not by individuals. In Ephesians we are told that individuals are built up and gifted so that they in turn can strengthen a body which is to do the work (*see* 4:16).

The Bible does not tell us much about organizational structures. Through the ages, the leaders of the Church have often disagreed on ecclesiastical structures or organizational relationships. But the Bible does have a good deal to say about the quality of relationships within its organizations. In fact, it goes so far as to assume that the key to organizational success lies in the *quality* of those relationships. Jesus told His disciples that men would know that they were His disciples by the quality of love they had for one another (*see* John 13:35). In His high priestly prayer, He even goes so far as to say that the basis of the world's belief in Him will derive from this oneness:

> [Jesus said:] "I do not ask in behalf of these alone, but for those also who believe in Me through their word; that they may all be one; even as Thou, Father, art in Me, and I in Thee, that they also may be in Us; that the world may believe that Thou didst send Me."
>
> John 17:20, 21

And although the Bible has its ringing command for service it seems much more concerned with how this service will be carried out (and how the people who carry it out will live with one another) than it is with how the work will be accomplished. Evidently, the work of Christ is to be done by the Church, caring for its members with the same concern that it has for the task it has been commissioned to do. And the Bible gives no simple answer as to when it is acceptable to sacrifice the good of the individual for the work of the local fellowship—or when aims of the fellowship are to be put aside for the good of the individual.

But we do have some models of people who are set aside for ministry. Certainly the commissioning of Paul and Barnabas in Acts 13:2 is an example. One can infer from this example that, from time to time, "healthy" people are to be sent out from the local fellowship and somehow given a different set of responsibilities. What does this have to say about Christian priorities as they apply to the individual and to the organization? We see three levels of Christian priority:

1. *Commitment to God and Christ.* This is of the highest priority. Everything begins here. It is a commitment so radical that Jesus demands that all other relationships be forfeited for it.
2. *Commitment to the Body of Christ (the Church).* This is a commitment as Christians one to another.
3. *Commitment to the work of Christ.* This is commitment to all the things we are called upon to do in His name.

Christian organizations and individuals ignore these priorities to their peril. After these commitments come all the rest of life.

To look at it another way, consider Figure 11. Here we have tried to show commitment to Christ as the foundation on which the relationships within the Church are built. It is on top of and flowing out of this superstructure that the work of Christ is established.

In our book *Strategy for Living,* we dealt with the implications of these three levels of priority for the Christian leader. We suggested that these priorities could be used to evaluate how one was spending one's life by examining one's use of time. Because the individual is a self-contained "organization," in many ways each one is much more able to keep these priorities straight than is the Christian organization.

HOW THE WORK GETS DONE

PRIORITIES OF COMMITMENT

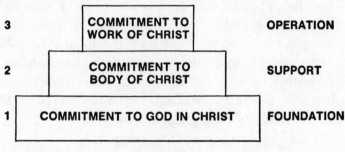

Figure 11

Priorities in Christian Organizations

From what the Bible tells us, there are no permanent answers to the dilemma of "building up the Body" and sending off the same people to carry out the work of Christ in the world. But it does appear that the Christian organization (as distinguished from the local church) has to put more weight in the direction of its goals.

Unlike the local church, the Christian organization begins from a different base. It is founded for a specific purpose. Unless it is primarily fellowship, this purpose is to carry out the *work,* although the dimension of fellowship will still be there. There are obvious expectations that one will experience Christian love and compassion. There is no question as to what comes first in the Christian organization: the *purpose* to which the organization is committed. The organization therefore accepts only "healthy" people. It recruits volunteers or paid-for people on the basis of what they can contribute to the purpose (work) of the organization.

Thus, the Christian organization must ultimately put the good of the organization over that of the individual. If an individual is unable to perform the task which the organization calls for him to do, the organization must replace that person with someone who is able. It is true, of course, that there are times in the everyday life of an organization when the business of the organization should be temporarily halted to care for the individual. But what we are speaking of here is the long-range and ultimate decision that must be made.

The local church does not have such a clear point of decision, since it has two seemingly irreconcilable goals: (1) caring for the individual in relationship to the Body of Christ; (2) doing the work of Christ. The local church cannot say to the individual, "We're sorry, friend, but you are no longer able to perform, and therefore you can no longer be a member of our organization."

There is a paradox to all of this. On the one hand, the individual is called upon to put the health of the Body and its individual members before the work of Christ. (The assumption here is that if the Body is healthy, the work of Christ will get done.) On the other hand, the group of individuals, the organization, must from time to time put what appears to be the immediate good of the individual aside for the good of the organization.

Recognizing the priorities. But having stated the paradox, what do we do? First, we must recognize the tension and our human limitations. There will be individuals in the organization who will come out on different sides of the question. People who are by nature task oriented will tend to put the task before relationships. On the other hand, people who are more concerned with relationships in life will tend to see these as the major emphases. There needs to be a continual reminder that there are no easy answers. This is part of our struggle to be Christians in a sinful world.

Second, we must hold up our highest priority—the Person of the Lord Jesus. We can become so busy with "doing" that we can forget the reason for it. The question should always be: "Will this bring glory to God?"

Functional priorities.   Having made this rather cursory venture into the general spiritual priorities of the organization, let us look at priorities among goals. Which goals have the highest priority? How do we keep on the right track?

- We can't minister to everyone. To whom do we want to minister?
- We can't do everything. What must we do first?
- We can't be everything. What is most important to be at this time?

Because both needs and situations change, these questions must be asked again and again. The cycle continues. We will face new problems and receive new information about the world in which we are working. Thus, we need to review our priorities continually.

Posteriorities. Organizations have a great deal of natural inertia. Once individuals have been assigned to a task, and suborganizations such as boards or committees or departments have been formed, the groups tend to generate lives of their own. It is easy to stop asking, "What is the goal of the Christian Education Committee this year?"—and start wondering, "What should we do this year?"

What we need are *posteriorities*, statements of things that we are *not* going to do this year. Picture an organization as an alligator—it has a great tendency to grow a very large tail. Periodically someone needs to chop off the tail, so the alligator can keep moving! Perhaps we need a committee to decide each year which 10 percent of all the things we did last year we are *not* going to do this year.

Further Reading

Make My Life a Miracle by Raymond C. Ortlund is an illustration of what happened when these priority principles were applied to a large church in Pasadena, California.

Strategy for Living by Ted W. Engstrom and Edward R. Dayton further develops the theme of priorities.

7

Planning to Do God's Work

[Jesus said:] "For which one of you, when he wants to build a tower does not first sit down and calculate the cost, to see if he has enough to complete it?"
Luke 14:28

Purposes and goals point direction. Priorities help us to choose which goals are most important. *Planning* is the stuff that converts goals into action and dreams into reality.

Planning As a Way of Life

An organization is like a raft floating in the river of history. In order to stay on course, to reach our destination in the future, we need to keep correcting. We note what has happened in the past and what we see ahead. Past history alone is inadequate to predict our future. There are just too many choices, too many different ways of doing things. The way we have done it in the past will seldom suffice for the future, since the past gives us inadequate controls. If we are guided only by the past, we are very much like the snail who backs his way across the pavement, trying to see where he has gone by watching his trail. The answer to the problem is planning.

Effective planning makes a statement about a desirable future, a statement of faith about a purpose or goal. It then seeks to determine the optimum steps (subgoals) needed to reach this goal or to recognize this purpose.

Long-range purposes and long-range goals determine general directions. Short-range goals become planning steps. As we have already seen, there is a relationship or interdependence between goals. We have to accomplish some goals in order to reach others and can break down all of our plans into these simple steps.

There is a close relationship between planning and problem solving. When we plan, we identify the goal we are attempting to meet. In problem solving, we decide what stands between us and the goal, so we can try to overcome the obstacle. The most effective problem solving is carried out when the problem is stated as a deviation from the goal: "We want to be *there*, but we're actually *here*. Therefore, we should do this . . . ." When goal setting and planning are a way of life, they can enhance an organization's effectiveness for a number of reasons.

First, the process of goal setting and planning can be the task around which people can focus their energies and thus build their relationships. There is nothing quite as satisfying as planning a future together, dreaming dreams, prayerfully considering what God would have us do and be. Without attempting to see the future, boards and committees have nothing to look forward to except more of the same. Futures become merely obligations rather than expectations.

Second, goal setting and planning can enhance communication about the life of the organization. When we begin to discuss possible futures, it is easier to accommodate to the present. Rather than talk about the mess we are in, we can lift our eyes to a day quite different from the one in which we find ourselves.

Third, because goals and plans are events that have not yet happened, they allow time for corrective action as new information and problems are encountered. When there is no opportunity to review our goals and make revised plans, we often are left with no time or no warning to take appropriate action.

For these reasons, we are led to espouse a theorem: *The ability of the Holy Spirit to operate within a local church or an organization is directly proportional to the amount of planning done.* What are we trying to say? When an organization has no goals and lives only from day to day, the only people who can use and direct it are those who have immediate information. Decisions must be made with very little information and very little consultation. However, when an organization stakes out a desirable future in terms of its goals and plans, all of its members have an opportunity to react with one another around those plans. There is time for reflection, time for reconsideration, time for the Holy Spirit to quietly do His office work.

It is not a question of whether we will or will not make plans. *Not to plan* is actually a plan in itself, for planning is attempting to decide in advance what we will and will not do in the next minutes, hours, days, months, or years. For the Christian organization, planning asks a question: "Will we affect the future at random or with purpose?" For affect it we will! We have the responsibility to decide what we should be or do, and therefore we must plan.

The Elements of Planning

In his very readable book *The Human Side of Planning,* David Ewing points out that planning has a generally poor track record. He's right! Ewing believes that the major difficulty has been the failure of planners to account for and take into their confidence the people for whom they are planning. But there is another side of the story. Many people's understanding of planning is narrow and confining. They picture plans as two high walls between which they must walk, and some Christians see such predetermined decisions as actually presumptuous affronts to God.

Planning starts with goals.   Planning must be based on measurable, accomplishable goals. It is not always easy to define clearly what we want to be or do, but the failure of many plans can be laid at the door of fuzzy goals. If our goals are clear and communicable, they will attract clear and communicable plans.

Planning is trying to write future history.   We are future-oriented beings. Although we plan on the basis of what we have perceived in the past, we try to project this understanding into the future. Except for the most simple, close-in projects, it is very unlikely that our predictions about the future will be 100 percent accurate. The old adage "If something can go wrong, it probably will!" is another way of saying that there are many more possibilities that something other than what we expected and hoped for will happen. The probability of things happening *our* way is remote.

From a Christian viewpoint, most of life is failure, since 99 percent is sin (missing the mark). Although we have learned that we live in an imperfect world, the unexpected or unpredictable keeps throwing us off balance. With planning, we attempt to wipe away some of the mist from the window of the future and reduce the number and impact of surprises. Planning is an attempt to move from "now" to "then"—to change from "things as they are" to "things as we want them to be." (See Figure 12.)

Planning as an arrow.   Since no man can be sure of the future, why plan? Basically, it is to improve the probability that what we believe should happen will happen. A future goal has been staked out in our minds: "To have a church membership of three hundred by 1980"—"To

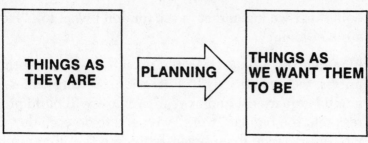

Figure 12

care for fifty children in Kenya during the next three years"—"To begin a new ministry in a ghetto area by June first." You name it! The point of the planning arrow figuratively touches the goal. The steps that need to be accomplished stretch along the path into the present to create a plan.

Planning as a process. If plans are considered as fixed and unchangeable, most likely they will fail. Planning is part of the growth process of an organization and is itself a process. The necessary steps are laid out, pointing toward the future goal; but as each major step is taken, reevaluation or feedback calls us to reexamine the future at each step and to measure the extent of our progress. If we have set a goal to have a hundred new members in our church during the next twelve months, we had better not wait until the eleventh month to see how we are doing. If we are planning to drive a thousand miles across unfamiliar territory, it is best to look at the road map once in a while to measure progress. If we plan to train a group for a new assignment and put them to work in six months, checkpoints along the way will be needed.

And yet, time and time again, we fail to evaluate progress. Sometimes we even set up an evaluation program and then fail to use it. Why? Many times it is because the measurement may take as much energy as the program itself. Other times we are so wrapped up in what we are doing that we just forget to ask (or don't want to), "How are we doing?"

Planning takes time.   Most of us will not take the time unless we consciously set it aside. Setting times of monthly, quarterly, and/or yearly review will build progress into the regular "work" we need to do each day. Of vital importance to an organization are the fifteen minutes of review which a leader takes with his or her secretary at the beginning of the day, the weekly staff meeting that summarizes what lies ahead, the quarterly evaluation meeting that reviews the previous three months (and looks at the goals for the next), and the annual planning time that reviews the past year's five-year plan and sets out a new one.

Because planning takes time, it should be begun as far in advance as possible. For example, a church should not wait until October to start planning the following year! The process should begin no later than April or May, so that as many people as possible can be brought in and neither people nor staff are rushed into the future.

The evaluation process should therefore be just as much a part of our planning as reaching the steps to the goal. We need to plan for the event of evaluation just as much as for any other event. Someone should be made responsible for the measurement (usually not the person responsible for the achievement).

Planning is people—or should be!   To go back to Ewing's observation, omitting the people part of the planning equation is courting disaster. Whenever possible, plans should be made by the people who are going to do the work. Thus, the task of a planning committee should not be to plan for other departments and committees, but rather to give them the needed information on which to base their plans and to give training, counsel, and/or coordination of planning.

Planning communicates intentions. As the population of the world increases—and our means of communicating with one another grow more sophisticated—the opportunities for working together grow at an ever-increasing rate. In the Western World, each of us plays a number of different roles in our private and organizational lives. Within an organization, we are leaders in one situation and followers in another, planners here and actors there. The number of "intersections" with other people's plans grows accordingly. It is as though the world were completely overlaid with side streets, highways, and expressways—each of them representing someone's (or some organization's) plans. If we are not clear in deciding where we are going and how we plan at present to get there, we will find ourselves continually colliding with other people's plans.

In the local church, it may be the failure of the choir director to communicate his plan for a children's festival at a time when the Sunday school was hoping to involve the same children in a new learning adventure. In the large organization, collisions may occur because one department has not adequately conveyed its intentions to use space, machine time, manpower. In an even larger context, one organization may move ahead with its plans without ascertaining the intentions of other organizations or sharing its own plans. The result is not only overlapping and duplication, but great confusion among those whom these different organizations are attempting to serve. How humorous yet tragic to discover that two churches on the same street in the same city plan to "have a Bible study in every city block by the end of next year."

By announcing our goals and clearly indicating the steps we currently plan to take, we establish clear-cut intersection points with others who are also making plans. As we noted before, we give the Holy Spirit the opportunity to work in everyone's mind and heart.

Further Reading

Parish Planning by Lyle E. Schaller is subtitled "How to Get Things Done in Your Church" and not only contains its own good bibliography, but is an excellent source book.

A Theology of Christian Education by Lawrence Richards contains much of the initial thinking that Richards covered in *A New Face for the Church*. This is helpful in analyzing ways in which the church can change and some directions in which it might move.

God's Purpose and Man's Plans by Edward R. Dayton. (See reading list for chapter 5.)

The Human Side of Planning by David W. Ewing is one of the few good books on planning that deals with all the obstacles to making good planning work for you. It lays out in honest detail the type of human interaction that is needed to implement any plan.

8

Stretching Into the Future

[Paul said:] But now, I am going to Jerusalem serving the saints . . . . Therefore, when I have finished this, and have put my seal on this fruit of theirs, I will go on by way of you to Spain.

Romans 15:25, 28

After the foregoing introduction to what planning is and what it can do for us, let us stretch our minds to the future and consider *long-range* planning.

Definitions

Long-range planning is usually limited to three to ten years. For most Christian organizations, perhaps five years is a good median position. Anything beyond ten years is so far in the future that our ability to predict it severely limits effective planning. On the other hand, if we do not move out at least three years into the future, we will get trapped into thinking about the future only on the basis of the present and even doing our planning on the basis of the past.

A good definition of long-range planning is "risk-taking decision making." Why *risk?* Since any statement about the future is a statement of faith, any decision based upon our perception of the future contains an element of risk, which is not necessarily something to be avoided. It is only by risking that we test our faith. What long-range planning attempts to do is to make decisions that will reduce the risk.

Why do we define long-range planning as risk-taking decision making? Because the daily life of the organization is ruled and regulated by the decisions it makes *today*. It is impossible to make binding decisions for tomorrow, but the decisions we make today have great impact upon tomorrow. In the main, our future is determined by *our* decisions, not other people's—although we are inclined to put the blame for our problems on outside circumstances, rather than accepting responsibility for our own actions. (Don't forget that *not* to make a decision is a decision in itself!)

Past decisions regulate our present behavior and, similarly, today's decisions will have a large impact on our future behavior. It is thus important to examine our past decisions and determine whether they are still effective. It is always possible to change a decision by making another one. Don't get locked into former decisions. As we increase our awareness of the decisions we have made (and are making), we will be able to make new decisions. Planning requires decisions—but we must not let an out-of-date decision hamper a future plan.

Long-range planning is not forecasting or trying to decide what will happen in the future. Forecasting is an extrapolation of the past into the present, based on the assumption that nothing else has changed or that things will continue on their present course. Planning seems to bring about change as well as to accommodate to it. In addition, long-range planning is not concerned with future decisions but with the future of present decisions.

Steps in Long-Range Planning

1. Clearly state the purposes of the organization. These may need to be identified in a general statement of faith and then broken down to specifics about particular purposes.

2. *Don't confuse the official organizational statement of faith with statements of purpose.* A statement of faith is the "why" of what we are doing. A statement of purpose gives the direction, the aim, the overall objectives. An organization may have more than one purpose or objective. For example, at the time of this writing, our organization had six major basic purposes: (1) ministering to children and families; (2) providing emergency aid; (3) developing self-reliance; (4) reaching the unreached; (5) strengthening leadership; (6) challenging to mission.

3. *Set both broad and specific goals to reach these purposes.* There may be some goals that are three or four years away. For example, a local church might have a goal of a certain number of members five years from now. If there are overseas projects, there may be a territorial goal, such as ministry in a given number of countries.

4. *Involve as many people as possible.* Long-range planning needs to be a top → down as well as a bottom → up affair. In other words, the objective is to bring all of the goals of the organization under its overall purposes. We want to make sure that all of our goals somehow relate to what we are trying to accomplish. One of the ways of heightening communication between the top leadership and the rest of the organization is to take everyone through the process. This is true for volunteer organizations as well as nonprofit service groups. (In Part III we will discuss some tools that you might use.)

5. *State your assumptions about the present and the future.* On the next page is a checklist of questions that you might want to answer:

- How long will there be a continuing need for our ministry?
- How do those who are benefited by our ministry feel about it?
- How will they continue to feel?
- What factors may eventuate to change our ministry?
- Will the world situation within which our ministry operates continue as it is, or become less or more stable? In what ways?
- Will there be a growing acceptance of our ministry?
- From whom can we expect the greatest support for our ministry?
- What are we assuming about the peoples among whom the ministry will be carried out?
- What type of people will we need for the future?
- Will they be available?
- What will be *their* needs?
- What are we assuming about the stability of our organization?
- Will it continue to have the same leadership five years from now? What might cause a change in this?
- Do we expect our organization to grow in size? In finances? In breadth of ministry?
- What will be the availability of finances?
- What will be the impact of inflation?
- What other possible economic factors will have an impact on our ministry?
- What are our theological assumptions?
- What are we assuming about the spiritual life of our people?
- What do we expect to happen to other organizations which are in a similar ministry?

These and many other assumptions will give you an understanding of what you really believe about the present and the future. Our failure to state assumptions often leaves us confused about the real meaning of our long-range plans. One way to build such a list of assumptions is to have different leaders in the organization complete the checklist and then compare the answers to see where clarification is needed.

6. *Develop realistic expectations.* What will happen if we *reach* our goals? One way of making a reasonable prediction is to write a scenario about the future. Some organizational leaders have found it useful to write a newspaper-type report dated five years in the future. They pretend that the five years are behind them and write a report about what has happened and how it came about. This kind of exercise will at times lead to some unexpected conclusions. But that is the very point! We are trying to remove as many surprises as possible from the future. This will help an individual as well as a group to communicate between different members of an organization.

7. *Study alternative courses of action.* There are always a number of different ways in which to go. Which are the most appropriate ones for you? This may require discussion and the eventual abandoning of a number of different plans. That's fine—better to fail on paper than in practice.

8. *Have the courage to make the necessary decisions.* Once you have decided upon a course, put it into action. Goals and plans are useless until executed. It often takes courage to step out in the simple trust that this is the way that God would have us go.

9. *Develop detailed plans or guidelines.* Detailed planning techniques to reach described objectives will be discussed in Parts II and III. Make sure that you have allowed enough time for each of the subgoals that you are going to pursue.

10. *Set dates when you will review your planning.* In other words, build this review into the planning as one of the subgoals or milestones. There must be continual review through analyzing results and evaluating whether we have reached forecasted milestones. If we have not, we need to take corrective action.

People and Organization Come First

The two most important things in long-range planning are people and organization—not money. A Christian organization, particularly the local church, tends to get bogged down by its concern for money and too often allows its planning to be done by its budgeting. Its vision may be limited by the amount of dollars it believes it can anticipate from its constituency. We need to see that—if the people have the skills, motivation, and the energy to carry out the task, and if they are given the adequate communication which should be provided— they can then overcome the problems of money. Material resources constitute just part of the elements of the overall task and should not be the controlling factor. Once we decide where we believe God wants us to go, we should use that same sanctified imagination to discover where the resources will come from.

In our opinion, there is too much emphasis today on the cost of raising money. It is true, of course, that there are many unscrupulous organizations that are raising money for their own use rather than for their advertised ministry, but it is just as true that it takes financial energy (money) to raise money. It seems like good stewardship to present a clear picture of what we believe God has called us to do—and to spend the money to communicate fairly the need as we see it.

Levels of Complexity

A good long-range planning program is one that meets the level of complexity of the organization. There is usually a direct correlation between the degree of complexity and the size of the organization (in terms of the number of people involved, rather than the amount of money in the budget). For some organizations, the steps that we have outlined above could be carried out by four or five people over a period of two or three days. In other organizations, the process might take a year.

Putting Planning to Work

Decide what kind of an organization God wants this to be. You cannot do everything. *What is it you want to do?* You cannot reach everyone. *Who is it you want to reach?* We cannot all have the same style of organization. *What kind of style should you have?* Set goals for your particular kind of outreach, community, and style.

Make a new three- to five-year plan each year. Long-range planning is a continuous process. This is a key idea. Too often people think that long-range planning is done every three to five years and is then used as a point of departure. This works for planning such static things as buildings. (In that case, we would hope that the plans would *not* be changing every year!) But when we are dealing with ministry to people, as are most Christian organizations, we should expect that change will come about. Planning is an arrow which points the direction to the future. The specifics need to be continually adjusted. There is much value in looking into the future, however, since long-range planning—

1. Gives an overall picture of where we believe we are going.

2. Helps to clarify our goals and find motivated people who will be attracted by those goals.

3. Helps to decide what we are *not* going to do and therefore keeps us from unknowingly drifting into some new area of ministry which detracts from the one we are already in.

4. Gives us an overview of our needed resources. It helps us to see not only what kind of resources we are going to need (so that we can plan and save for them), but also how effective these resources may be in the future.

5. Helps us to prepare for the unexpected because it assumes that the unexpected will happen and tries to keep the organization flexible enough to change quickly to meet new situations.

Focus Your Planning

Set a few overarching goals for each year.   Build your program around them, since there are few things more debilitating than having too many competing goals. Too often in the local church we seem to have a new emphasis every month. Perhaps there should be just one major emphasis for the current year, with the emphasis for the following years well displayed in our plans. (If people want to know why we aren't doing their special project, we can point to the future and say, "*Next* year! And we need *you* to help plan it.")

Let the needs, purposes, goals, and plans dictate the program and organizational structure.   Don't get trapped into "functional obsolescence." Too many organizations are made up of committees and structures which were appropriate five years before but which are no longer necessary. Instead of letting the goals dictate the organizational structure, such groups have let the structure dictate the goals. A good example would be a typical Christian-education committee in a local church. The way the committee was formed may well have met the needs ten years ago. Now the committee finds itself trying to justify its existence by deciding what it will do during this coming year—when the important thing is to look at the overall purpose and long-range goals of the organization and then decide what kind of committee is needed at this time.

Further Reading

The Human Side of Planning by David W. Ewing. (See reading list for chapter 7.)

9

Problem Solving

*Do you not know that those who run in a race all run,
but only one receives the prize? Run in such a way
that you may win.*

1 Corinthians 9:24

We have worked through the various steps of our organizational cycle as though they were separable and abstract, yet remembering that they are closely intertwined. Now we have moved from the business of thinking about what to do—and getting ready to do it—to the actual doing. This should involve trying to accomplish what we have planned to do with the resources we have gathered. Our desire is to reach our goals—*to make our goals past events*, things that have happened. However, as we have often noted, the future seldom conforms to our plans. We live in times in which it is impossible to take into account many of the future events that will face us. For an enterprise of any size, there will always be the need to take corrective action as we act upon our plans. To a large degree, this is what "management" is all about. We discuss in our book *The Art of Management for Christian Leaders* many of the managerial skills you will need if you are a leader of a Christian enterprise. In this section we focus on the need for problem solving—the need to overcome the obstacles that are bound to lie in our path as we try to go through this process of goals, priorities, planning, and managing.

Planning vs. Problem Solving

There is a close relationship between planning and problem solving. In each case, there is recognition that action is required and a variety of approaches to carry out that action. There is an element of doubt about the outcome, since we cannot predict what the future will be like. There is also the element of time needed to carry out the action. Finally, there is the recognition that there are a number of steps necessary for a successful action.

What, then, is the difference between planning and problem solving? Basically, planning has to do with deciding on a course of action to reach a goal. It is an attempt to write future history. Problem solving is an attempt to understand what keeps us from reaching a goal and what step (or new steps) we have to take in order to reach it. Another way of saying this is that when we think about "planning," we are assuming that we have a great deal of the future still before us. Problem solving has a "nowness" about it. There is a need *right now* to overcome an obstacle that lies in our path. It is probably this factor of timeliness that basically differentiates problem solving from planning, although the steps to both are quite similar.

The basic steps to problem solving are:

1. Understand what needs to be done.
2. Compare the task or problem with known experience.
3. Devise an overall strategy or approach.
4. Make a plan to solve the problem.
5. Gather resources to carry out the plan.
6. Carry out the plan.
7. Use the results.

It is immediately obvious that this sequence is very similar to the organizational cycle. This should not surprise us. After all, solving the "big problem"—reaching the major goals of the organization—is probably quite similar to solving the "small problem"—how to get out of the mess we are in right now.

1. Understand what needs to be done. There is an adage that "understanding what needs to be done is half the solution." (There is another adage that "knowing it *can* be done is half the solution." With those two it looks like we're almost home!) This understanding of what needs to be done is not as simple as it may seem. Problems usually arrive well disguised as something quite different. Many times you first become aware of them when someone comes rushing into your office with a statement that "something has to be done about . . . !" That "something" may be too many cars in the parking lot, the morning service not starting on time, missionaries on the field not receiving their monthly allowances on schedule—or even a major war in Africa. But how does that problem relate to you and your organization? Is it really *your* problem, and is it really *the* problem? How do you find out?

Attempt to state the problem as a deviation from a goal. This is the first step. After all, if the situation is not keeping you from reaching one of your goals, is it really *your* problem? Many times this leads you to state some new subgoal that you did not realize you had or needed. It was just something that you had not taken into account in your planning. In other words, it is not very worthwhile to identify what you wanted to happen that is *not* happening—or what *is* happening that you did not want to happen!

State the problem in writing. Now, there are many problems that the manager's experience permits him to handle quickly and without a great deal of detailed planning. However, we cannot overemphasize the value of framing the problem in words that will communicate meaningfully to others and yourself. Another helpful factor involved here is that you need to *take time*—to slow down and really understand what is going on. We usually have more time to solve a problem than we lead ourselves to believe. The more thought that you can give before acting, the more likely you will deal with the problem as effectively as you can.

What are some of the factors that you need to note down? Ask yourself some questions: How did we first learn about this problem? How accurate is our information? How serious is the problem? How much time do we have to solve the problem? (This is probably the most important question.)

Break the problem down into its logical elements. For example, suppose that your problem is one of parking. Let us assume that you are working in a local church. You have planned a new outreach which is attracting a number of additional people to the Sunday-morning service, but you forgot to take into account the problem of where these people would park. The situation is that on Sunday morning the thirty parking spaces are being overwhelmed with sixty automobiles, carrying a hundred and sixty people. What are the elements of this problem?

First, there is the element of space. (You have thirty spaces on the church grounds.) Second, there is the element of the number of cars. (You have thirty spaces, but sixty cars.) Third, there is the element of the number of people riding in those cars. (As best as you can tell, there are a hundred and sixty people arriving in sixty cars— less than three per car.) Fourth is the element of time. (These people are all arriving between 10:50 and 11:00 A.M. There is only one church service.)

Now go further into your analysis of each of these elements, doing your best to try to describe the components of each. Is there a possibility of getting more parking space on the grounds? Is there some way that we can get people to come at different times? What is the major cause of the problem? What would the situation be like if the problem did not exist? Would this be a desirable situation? These and many other questions—with answers written down—will really help you and others to understand the problem. In all of this writing down, many things are going on. You are not only helping yourself and others to understand, but at the same time you are giving yourself and others training in problem solving, while providing some kind of record of your thought processes. At the end of this chapter is a suggested form which might be of help in understanding and organizing the approach to problem solving. It can be adapted to the specific needs of any problem at hand.

2. *Compare the task with known experience.* Our entire perception of the future is and must be based upon our perception of the past. When we talk about "using our experience" to solve a problem, we are talking about using past happenings to help us in the future. It may be somebody else's experience that has been written down in a book or that we have heard about in some other way. The main thing to remember is to begin by assuming that somebody else has had this problem and probably has solved it. Surprisingly, much can be done with a few phone calls to ask other people whether they (or someone they know) have had a similar problem.

Ask yourself such questions as: "Do we know of an approach that has worked before?" or "Has someone else had a problem which was close enough to ours that we think using that approach might be a good way to go?" On the other hand, do we know of some approaches that we (or others) have tried and found to be harmful, that not only have not worked, but that have set us back further than we were before? As an example in our parking problem, somebody might have once attempted to start charging people to park in the church parking lot on Sunday morning—only to discover that although the parking spaces were not filled, the number of people in church dropped dramatically!

A third kind of experience from the past is one which is neither helpful nor harmful. It is useless and neither advances us nor puts us back. For example, someone might once have suggested a set of car pools, only to discover that this just did not fit the life-style of our congregation. Nobody got angry about it, but it didn't help our problem either.

Gather as much information as you can. Most of the time, in the very business of understanding the problem, the solution will become obvious. As we have said before, what appears to be a step-by-step, logical process on paper does not usually go on inside our heads in the same "logical" way.

If we have no previous experience at hand for this particular problem, we may have to do "research." A simple definition of research is "an attempt to supply missing experience." Most research is carried out to learn something that will further mankind and may be either very formal or informal. Thus, when we start calling other local churches to ask them about *their* parking problems, we are involved in research.

3. *Devise an overall strategy or approach.* A strategy is an overview of how we will go about something. In one sense, it defines the things that we are not going to do and the approaches that we are not going to take. It is not a detailed plan in itself, but is rather a description of how we are going to go about solving the problem.

Let us say that for our parking problem our overall strategy was to have the regular members of the church not use the parking lot. The steps that we would go about to get them to leave the parking spaces for visitors would be part of our detailed plan.

If we have a complicated problem, our strategy will be correspondingly more complicated. The usefulness of a strategy statement is to communicate to one another what our general approach is going to be and to help people understand those things which we have decided not to do.

4. *Make a plan to solve the problem.* Having decided upon an overall strategy and selected an approach based on previous experience or research, the time has come to make a decision to move ahead. This is not always as easy as it sounds. Many times we will be faced with the need to make a very difficult decision. As we mentioned when we discussed long-range planning, there is an element of risk involved. In our example, just about the time we are ready to execute our plan, we may begin to wonder whether some of the old-timers in the church will really go along with it. Don't let such feelings immobilize you. Use them to help you foresee other obstacles that you may need to overcome before you can move ahead.

Once the decision is made, the next step is to try to set subgoals for the different elements involved. In our example, we have already broken down the problem into elements of parking spaces, automobiles, people, and time. It is obvious that we must set a goal so that people either leave their cars home or are provided with other suitable parking places. We may have to set some goals for *when* we expect these people to arrive at church. For example, if we are going to ask the regular members to park some distance from the church, we must set a goal to try to have them leave home earlier.

At this point, people very often leave out a key part of the planning process by forgetting to plan on how they will evaluate success. In our example, this evaluation is pretty straightforward. We can stand by the parking lot and notice how many cars arrive! However, even in this simple situation, we may need somebody on subsequent Sundays to determine if the solution is working or if some new problem is arising. In other words, there are two evaluations to be made. We first evaluate whether our approach to the problem is working. Second, we evaluate whether we have actually met the goal. By building in the evaluation as one of the planned elements, we insure that we will not continue along a course of action that is either useless or harmful.

Having made a plan, we need to go through the regular steps of estimating the time needed for each step, the money (budget), the facilities for each step (resources), and the people (organization). If one of our estimates indicates that our plan will not work, we then need to replan or seek another solution, which may eventually mean modifying the goal. A lot of people get hung up at this point. They wonder about the sense of going through all this writing things down—only to discover that they won't work. What's the point?

A story is told about Thomas Edison, who invented (among other things) the electric light bulb. As we know, the principle of the light bulb is that when a current is passed through a resistant material, the material gets very hot and glows, creating a light. The difficulty is that certain materials quickly burn up, even if kept in a vacuum where there is no oxygen. It took Thomas Edison a long time to discover this, and along the way he experimented with many different materials. One night, so the story goes, he returned home and announced to his wife that he "just finished the ten thousandth experiment!"

"Did it work?" she queried.

"Nope."

"Aren't you discouraged?" she asked.

"Discouraged? We now know ten thousand ways that won't work!"

Well, Edison's way is one way—but maybe it is easier to fail on paper than through thousands of experiments.

5. Gather resources. It is useful to remember that everything that has taken so long to describe may happen very quickly. You may have arrived at the plan to solve your parking problem within fifteen minutes after it was first announced to you. On the other hand, a week longer may have gone by while you discussed it with different people. Again, this will depend upon the seriousness of the problem with respect to time.

Now comes the moment to begin to put the plan into action. The same cycle that we saw before in the total organization begins to take effect. We now need to gather the resources and organize them for action. There will be finances to be involved, tasks to be assigned, and facilities to be allocated.

For example, let us assume we decided to have signs painted at the two entrances of our parking lot, indicating that the lot was reserved for handicapped persons, senior citizens, or visitors to the church—and announcing that others were asked to park elsewhere. There also might have been a need to print up a flyer to be given out to church members a week or two ahead of time, identifying the location of other places where friendly merchants would allow church parking on Sunday mornings. There were probably some staff people who were involved. Perhaps a task force was appointed to pull all this together and to be there on Sunday mornings to direct people to the proper place. There had been the merchants to be contacted for permission to use their parking lots—as well as some kind of program to encourage people to walk that extra five minutes as part of their contribution towards the outreach of the church.

6. Carry out the plan. As we begin to put the plan into action, we need to measure results continually, starting at the beginning. It may be too late to wait until Sunday morning to find out that people are not paying any attention to our signs. We may have to take some earlier action within the congregation to find out if people will be accepting of this. We may be able to discover how many people plan to use the outlying parking facilities rather than the church facility on the following Sunday.

No doubt we will run into problems. Perhaps the merchant who has made available his lot forgets that he has planned a Sunday sale that particular day. Somebody had better be ready with a contingency plan! Perhaps we discover that the instructions that we thought were so clear have turned out to be obscure and needing correction. Perhaps we discover that people who have been coming to the church for two or three Sundays don't consider themselves "visitors" anymore—and now *everybody* is parking outside the church parking lot, giving it a very empty look!

Another factor that we need to take into account as we carry out the plan is to consolidate our gains. Too often in Christian work we fail to plan for success. We plan an evangelistic campaign and expect to have a hundred people make a decision for Christ, but provide only two counselors. When people are performing according to our hopes and expectations, they need to be affirmed in what they are doing. We need to congratulate those people who have parked in the outlying parking lots, even while we assure visitors that they are welcome to use the main lot. Be ready for success. It does come!

Finally, when the results match the definition of our goal—when the number of empty spaces on Sunday morning is what we hoped for—we have reached our goal and have solved our problems.

7. *Use the results.* It is surprising how often, after we solve the problem, we do not continue to take advantage of the gains that we have made. It may take six months before church members get in the habit of parking outside the parking lot. There is probably going to be a need for continuing reminders and affirmation of people who cooperate. In other words, we need to remind people that the goal is part of a larger task—the parking problem is really not the basic one. Our basic problem was that not enough people were coming to church. What we were trying to do was to alleviate one of the conditions that kept them from coming. What else can we do to foster church growth?

We need to make sure to remember what we have learned. Once we have done something well, we need to celebrate that victory and use it to give us the confidence to take on new problems.

Guide for Problem Solvers

Below is a suggested *Guide for Problem Solvers*. Adapted to individual needs and situations, it can be an invaluable tool. Italicized "answers" illustrate its use on one specific problem, broadly stated as the need for adequate parking space (to encourage new-member church attendance).

A. Understanding the Problem

What seems to be the situation? *We don't have enough parking spaces.*

What goal is this problem keeping us from achieving? *Our desire to have new members come to our church.*

How do we know that this is really the situation? *We can see the parking lot on Sunday morning.*

How accurate is my information? *Quite accurate.*

How much time do we have to solve the problem? *One to two months.*

How serious is it? *Very serious if we really want to see our church grow.*

Can we break it down into different components? *(1) Parking spaces; (2) number of cars; (3) number of people; (4) time.*

Who are the people involved? *The congregation and the church board.*

Whose mind, attitude, or behavior has to be changed to solve the problem? *The congregation and the church board.*

B. Compare the Task With Known Experience

Have we ever seen a problem like this before? *No. Our recent church growth is a new phenomenon to us.*

Who else might have or has had the same problem? *Other churches who are growing as we are.*

Is there a solution to another problem that might work for this one? *Not that we can think of.*

Do we know of attempted solutions to this problem that have been useless or harmful? *(1) Trying to make parking spaces smaller; (2) spending a lot of money on parking.*

How can we go about getting more information on possible solutions? *Telephone the three other growing churches in our area.*

C. Devise an Overall Strategy

What is our general approach to solving the problem? *Find alternate parking and convince the congregation to use it.*

What are we *not* going to do? *Add another service.*

D. Make a Plan to Solve the Problem

What are the different elements of the problem and the goal for solving each one? *(1) Ten empty spaces on Sunday morning; (2) most of the congregation using different lots.*

What steps need to be taken to reach each of these goals? *(1) Find alternate parking; (2) motivate the congregation to use the alternate parking.*

When will each step need to be accomplished? *Four weeks from now.*

Who will be responsible for the overall and each step? *Chairman: Bill Brown. Committee: Burns, Rogers, and Stearn.*

How much will it cost? *$39.00 for leaflets and signs.*

How will we measure progress against our solution? *Observation each Sunday.*

Do we have the people, resources and courage to carry out this approach? *Yes.*

E. **Gather Resources**

People recruited? *Bill Brown, Burns, Rogers, Stearn.*

Schedules set? _____

Goals agreed upon? _____

Resources allocated? _____

F. **Carry Out the Plan**

How are we doing against each phase? *First Sunday: 2 empty spaces; second Sunday: 5 empty spaces; third Sunday: 15 empty spaces.*

What corrective action needs to be taken? *First Sunday: additional encouragement to the congregation and information on alternate lots.*

How can we consolidate the gains we have made? *Keep affirming those who are walking from some distance.*

G. **Use the Results**

Who needs to be congratulated? *The committee and the congregation.*

Now that we have solved the problem, how is our program really better? *New members are coming to our church.*

Has the real problem been solved? *Yes.*

What have we learned to keep us from repeating the problem? *As new members join the church, they need to be encouraged to park in the alternate lot provided by friendly merchants.*

What have we learned that will help us solve other problems? *People will cooperate if they see a real need and it is adequately communicated.*

How can we communicate what we have learned to ourselves and others? *Call the other churches that we asked information from and tell them how we solved the problem.*

Further Reading

The Rational Manager by Charles H. Kepner and Benjamin B. Tregoe sets forth a systematic approach to problem solving and decision making. Describes procedures for analyzing problems, making decisions, and preventing potential problems.

Analyzing Performance Problems; or, You Really Oughta Wanna by Robert F. Mager and Peter Pipe effectively applies principles of human behavior and provides a procedure for analyzing problems. Practical.

God's Purpose and Man's Plans by Edward R. Dayton. (See reading list for chapter 5.)

Part II

Putting Basic Concepts to Work

10 Where Are You Now?
11 Where Do You Begin?
12 An Overall Approach
13 A Case Study

10

Where Are You Now?

The plans of the diligent lead surely to advantage . . . .

Proverbs 21:5

Organizations are formal relationships between a group of people who share a common purpose. We have attempted to describe them in chapter 2. How formal these relationships become, what rules and regulations are established, and what hierarchies are built will vary with time and size. Organizations may last for a few minutes—or a lifetime.

The Organizational Cycle

Let us review what we covered in chapter 4. In one way or another, all organizations go through the same cycle (see Figure 13) of seeing a need they feel should be met and deciding to do something about it—they state their *purpose*. But purposes turn out to be rather intangible at times, so the next step is to decide how the world will be different as a result of their efforts—*goals* are set. Since they usually have more things that they would like to change than are possible, they have to select from their many possible goals those that are the most important, those they value the most—*priorities* are established. Having for the moment some picture of the desired future, an organization then sets about trying to figure out the best way to reach those goals, the steps it

111

should follow: it does some *planning*. Once plans are made, the organization sets about bringing together the necessary resources and people and goes about the business of trying to reach the goal—it takes *action*. Since the future is seldom exactly the way we imagine it, difficulties will occur—the organization soon finds itself *correcting* its course to fit the current situation. Hopefully, goals are eventually reached (either as originally stated or in modified form)—now is the time for *evaluation* of the goals, the plans, and the resources used. This evaluation will in turn be profitable as the organization repeats the cycle and sets new goals.

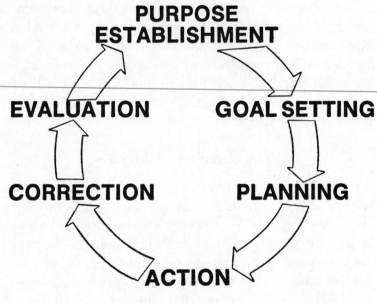

Figure 13

This cycle is applicable to the entire organization and its subcomponents: the committees, departments, commissions, and task forces within the organization. Among the advantages of picturing this repetitive organizational growth cycle is that it:

1. Allows different members and groups of the organization to visualize not only where they are but where others are.
2. Helps groups within the organization to communicate where they are and where they are going.
3. Puts the emphasis on what is eventually to be accomplished, rather than how it is to be accomplished or through what organizational form.
4. Pictures the organization as being in the process of moving ahead, rather than existing in a static state.

For example, ten people who are forming a new church can thus better visualize what lies ahead and what they have to do to realize the future to which they believe God is calling them. A mission field office can set its goals and have a way of sharing (with both the field staff and the home office) where it has been, where it is now, and where it is going. A large Christian service organization can use the same cycle for its corporate goals and fit the subgoals of its various divisions into the cycle.

But most people don't talk about organizations this way. They discuss organization charts, key people, buildings, past accomplishments, maybe even future goals, although too often these goals tend to be static things such as a new building project or field site. The aim of Part II is to help people see intellectually what happens in the life of an organization and to enable them to experience this process in a dynamic way.

Be an Agent for Change

You may be a pastor trying to get a handle on your congregation. Or you may be an executive in a mission agency, a field leader, or the head of a small department. Regardless of your position, if you encourage a new order of things and attempt some new ways of thinking and eventually doing, you are an agent for change.

People only like to change when they are discontented. It may be a broad and holy discontent, leading to a wish to see the world a more God-honoring place—or it may be a desire to remove a minor discomfort or annoyance. As Sol Alinsky, the famous union organizer, used to say, "Rub the bruises sore!" He was focusing on the fact that you have to begin with the discontent and build on that.

We are not advocating that you start moving through your organization and starting a lot of trouble. We are suggesting that you have to find those people who have the same desire to see things done more effectively, to accomplish more and reach higher goals. They will not always be a part of the official hierarchy.

The other side of the coin is that there will also be people who are completely content. They will view negatively any change, even a new way of thinking. As Machiavelli, counselor to statesmen, observed in *The Prince* (1532): "There is nothing more difficult to carry out, nor more doubtful of success, nor more dangerous to handle than to initiate a new order of things."

Making good goals our goals.   Again, a helpful insight as we begin this journey into the future is to realize that good goals are *our* goals—bad goals are *their* goals! We are all familiar with the "they" or "them" of everyday conversation. *They* kept it from happening. *They* are the ones who are always causing trouble. *They* should have done it another way. It never would have happened that way if it weren't for *them.* Therein lies the wonder and power of shared goals. To have a common goal and purpose with another human being does more to build understanding than any amount of *planned* fellowship. To feel that you are on the outside looking at someone else's goals raises all kinds of negative feelings.

As you set about discovering where you and your organization are, take people along with you from the beginning. Although it is exciting to discover something all by yourself, such excitement is not lasting and is difficult to share. In the long run, the memories that please us most are memories of times when we have done things together. So take your time. (We'll say that a number of times along the way!) You may have to take some side journeys to share some others' goals, but if they rejoin you on the royal highway that leads you to God's good goals for your organization, it will be well worth it.

Spun Out or in Orbit?

As you think about the theoretical organizational cycle, how would you say your organization is doing? Is it still in orbit, still going through this cycle? Is it going through the cycle at all levels of the organization? In other words, does the overall organization see this as a process which it uses, one that is well understood by the different committees or departments of the organization? Or has your organization spun out of orbit somewhere along the way?

Spinout can occur at a number of places. If it occurs in the initial planning stage, the organization never really comes into being. We are all familiar with bull sessions by two or three people, most of which begin with such expression as: "Wouldn't it be great if . . . ?" Spinout can also occur at the planning stage the second time around. This is much more likely to happen if an organization has been initially successful. Its members may now believe that they already know how to do something and therefore don't need to plan. Spinout at the planning stage can occur with growth. What was once an adequate planning system (carried out within the head of one or two people at the early stages of an organization) is no longer adequate. The planning system must be formalized, and failure to do this will cause spinout.

Even if the organization has gotten into the action phase, it can still spin out of the cycle. We mentioned earlier that often one of the most dangerous threats to organizational welfare is initial success. If things go very much as planned, there is a tendency to believe that the initial actions are the way to do it now: "But we've *always* done it that way!"

The next place where the organization can spin out of orbit is in failure to take corrective action. Perhaps the initial action was "good," but not really good enough. Instead of changing the original plans, correcting to do better, the organization may be satisfied to reach only some of its goals. There is a great tendency for Christian organizations to fall back on "God's will" as their reason for failure. We have no way of reconciling this kind of response. Obviously, we must remain in the tension that as our hearts are corporately tuned to God's will, He will be working good through us. In that sense, all things that happen to us are God's will. But on the other side of tension (or the paradox) is the fact that everything we do is in some way our responsibility. We have been commanded to act—and therefore are responsible.

Some organizations spin out further along in the cycle because they never really institute an evaluation process. If this is not done, they probably do not have a formal plan in process. In other words, they did the initial planning—necessary to get them under way—but they never formalized this in a way that called themselves to account. Such organizations have neither yearly nor semi-yearly times of evaluation nor planning cycles that they go through every year. They may, however, have a budgeting cycle. Most organizations do face up to the fact that they need to have money to survive, and they have to acquire it in some particular way. A great deal of planning may be done automatically by "extrapolation of the budget."

Some of the questions that you might ask in order to ascertain where your organization is are covered in the checklist below. Visualize organizational differences by seeing the cycle for a growing organization as an ever-widening circle. The steps are the same, but get more difficult and complex as the circle gets larger. The absence of any one step can be increasingly more destructive to the organization.

Organizational Life Cycle Checklist

____ Does the organization have a clear statement of its purpose and objectives?

____ Are the overall goals within the organization clearly announced and apparent to the key people?

____ Does each group have its own specific goals?

____ Is there an overall picture of how the goals of the subgroups fit into the goals of the overall organization?

____ Does the organization have a sense of priorities? In other words, does it understand what it is *not* going to do, as well as what it *is* going to do?

____ Is there a part of the organization that has been specifically assigned the task of overall, corporate planning (such as a planning committee, management committee) or another group that has the goal of making sure that the organization does planning each year?

____ Is the organization growing in its effectiveness—by whatever measure it may use?

____ Has the organization a formal training program for its people?

____ Are the means and methods of the organization changing with the times? In other words, if the organization is more than five years old, is it using different means and methods from those with which it began?

____ Is the organizational structure continually being reviewed to see if it fits the current goals of the organization?

—— Is there someone (or a subgroup) responsible for evaluating progress against goals?

Situation Analysis

Assuming that you have some initial feeling of whether your organization is moving, is static, or is slipping behind in the organization cycle, where do you go from here?

It is important to see that organizations are made up of different components of their past, present, and future. In one sense, organizations can be viewed as being in continual tension between these components. In Figure 4 (see chapter 2), we tried to show the organization as suspended between its past—its *history;* its present—its *commitments* and the *situation* in which it finds itself; and its future—its *goals.* This model is a useful analysis tool.

History—the past. Some organizations will have a short history and some will have a long one. Some will be very conscious of their history, and others will not think too much about it. You may remember the song from the musical *Fiddler on the Roof.* When asked why things were done a certain way in the village, the answer was "Tradition!" A great deal of the things done in organizations are in this same category. However, we are no longer a "traditional" society, but rather one in which tradition is no longer a necessary platform on which to build all of the future. It is helpful to see how dependent the organization is on its tradition and history. Traditional thinking might be indicated by any of the following:

- A yearly celebration of some historical event is held within the organization.
- A great deal of emphasis is put on the organization's yearly anniversary.

- There are formalities not written into any procedures but which are carried out repeatedly. In a local church, this might be the way weddings are conducted. In a mission, this might have to do with the way people are commissioned for their overseas assignments.
- Written policies and by-laws have been unchanged over the past five years.
- There are a number of organizational members who were there "at the beginning" and who still tend to dominate the future of the organization.
- Members of the middle management of the organization are in their fifties or sixties.
- A book or other formal history of the organization has been written (either about the organization or about its founder).
- The organization is more than twenty-five years old.

Commitments and situation—the present. We can have many types of *commitments,* some more visible than others. For example, we may have a financial commitment to a lending institution. We will have commitments to our staff in forms of such things as retirement plans or health plans, as well as moral and ethical commitments that we have made as part of the staff adjoined to the organization. We may have implied commitments to our donors or members of an organization. When we offered a particular kind of program which they agreed to support, we became committed to do our best to complete the program in the manner in which we described it to our constituency. There may be commitments to the community in which we live, such as taxes and social and community obligations. Many organizations have commitments to other organizations, agreements which they need to honor. This is particularly true of service organizations.

At a more intrinsic level, an organization may have a commitment to excellence, to doing things as well as it possibly can. Certainly the Christian organization should have a commitment to bring glory to God and to do everything possible to carry out its ministry in a way that will honor Him.

At the other side is the present *situation*—the environment in which we find ourselves. Unfortunately, this is the place at which most organizations focus a great deal of attention when they are trying to analyze where they are. Certainly such information is important. It is important to know about the neighborhood in which we might be ministering, the effect of our ministry, our income, the number of members—the demographics of our situation. But we usually do not need anywhere near as much data as most people gather. Probably the greatest benefit of gathering a lot of data about the present situation is to help us learn together, so that when we build goals and plans, they are good goals—*our* goals. By getting members of the organization involved in the data-gathering process, new insights into the effectiveness of the organization can be encouraged, insights that would not have been gained or accepted in any other way.

Goals—the future.   To keep the organization in proper balance or creative tension, we need goals that pull us into the future. By listing the goals of the organization as we understand them, we can gain a balanced understanding of the present situation.

Where Are You Now?

On four sheets of paper list a summary of your organization's *history, commitments, situation,* and *goals* as best you understand them. Now review your answers to the checklist which begins on page 117.

Where are you?

Further Reading

The Art of Getting Your Own Sweet Way by Philip B. Crosby may not sound like a book for *Christian* leaders. However, Crosby's situation analysis is a very effective tool for trying to understand the kind of situation that you're in and planning your way out of the problem. The Crosby approach to situation management is worth the price of the book

11

Where Do You Begin?

For no man can lay a foundation other than the one which is laid, which is Jesus Christ.

1 Corinthians 3:11

Let us assume that you, as a leader, have done some thinking and talking about your organization and believe that it needs to be strengthened. Let us assume further that you accept the concept of the organizational life cycle and would like to see your organization following this pattern in an overt and understandable way.

Establishment of Goals

How can you use this idea of the organizational life cycle to put your desires to work? Perhaps you quickly respond, "To start with, I guess I'd better decide on the organization's goals."

The difficulty with that response is that *you* are deciding for the organization. If you begin here, you may quickly discover that "good goals are *your* goals and bad goals are *their* goals!" No, your first goal is to see the process working, not to decide on the outcome. This may be hard for a leader to accept. After all, isn't it the job of a leader to lead? Yes, but if you believe that—in a Christian organization—the Holy Spirit indwells all the members, and the same Holy Spirit is willing and able to shape them into a body, you have to allow Him the opportunity to work.

123

The purpose of the organization is probably already set. What we are after is the establishment and effective carrying out of goals which will support that purpose. It may feel a lot more comfortable if things are done *your* way, but as you learn to live more and more with "our" way (the way of the group) you will discover that there is wisdom in many counselors, if that wisdom can be prayerfully channeled. The first point is:

POINT 1: Assume that you will be part of the process and allow yourself to be led by it. Don't ask other people to submit to something to which you are not willing to submit yourself.

The ideal situation would be that sometime in the future every member would have a clear understanding of the goals for the organization, have an idea as to where they fit and how they contribute to these goals, and believe that these are good, honorable, and retainable goals. It is unlikely that in an organization of any size you will ever reach that ideal. But this leads us to the next point:

POINT 2: As you think ahead and move through the process, do your best to involve an ever-increasing number of people in the organization. People are most likely to be enthusiastic about goals and plans that they believe they have either had a part in planning or had a chance to review.

Getting the Process Moving

Both of us are members of the same large church. Until quite recently, when a congregational meeting was held, the first order of business was to elect a moderator. This was usually done quickly. A well-known member of the church was usually nominated and elected unopposed for this position. To the outsider it appeared as though the procedures were preplanned. They weren't, but it seemed that way—for in most congregational meetings the order of business moved right along with little opposition. One might have wondered why we went to all the trouble to agree to something that appeared to be already decided. The important thing to see here is that people are being given the *right to veto.* If the leaders of the congregation have done a good job of sensing the needs and desires of the people and have done their homework, there will be little or no opposition. People will have questions, but they will tend to be helpful. On the other hand, if the leaders take a sudden turn in the road and leave the congregation to one side, there are checks and balances that go to work. It is these which give people a sense of participating. As we will see, there are ways of getting many people involved earlier than the time of a final vote by a board or a congregation.

Move slowly. If you want to see some change, if you are discontented with the status quo, you already have the motivation to get something started. You may be impatient to begin. But . . .

POINT 3: Take your time. You may be way ahead of the people who need to be part of the process. We usually greatly overestimate what we can do in one year and very much underestimate what we can do in five.

In fact, you can use your reticence to move ahead to your advantage. If people accept a goal, they are usually impatient to get going. By allowing others to push you, you don't have to do all the pulling! Remember, the role of a planner is to help others discover their own plans.

Motivation. This is a good point to summarize some of the things that we have said about motivation. In one sense we know very little about what motivates people, although we know quite a bit about what *de*-motivates them. These are things which Frederick Herzberg calls "hygienic elements." People are *de*-motivated by poor working conditions, inadequate reward, and a number of environmental factors. But some things *do* motivate people in an organization.

1. Everyone is already motivated by something. The goals that motivate us are "good" goals which we see as *our* goals (as contrasted to *their* "bad" goals).

2. A corollary to this is that people are motivated by things which they help to formulate. There is a sense of *ownership* in what's going on. People are able to say, "That's *my* organization, carrying out *my* good desires."

3. People are motivated to support an organization in which they sense they have a stake, or at least the ability to exercise some control over the destiny of the organization. This is why most of us have such a strong desire to "know what's going on around here."

The implications from all of this are that any process designed to move an organization ahead needs to take *people* into account. Since most Christian organizations are in the "people business," these especially have to consider not only the people on staff who are doing the work, but also the people who support their work and those to whom and for whom they are ministering.

Entry Points

In the next chapter we will outline a systematic approach to the operation of the organizational cycle. But before such an approach is formalized, there usually needs to be some entry point to raise the consciousness level of the people involved, a way of beginning that will help people get moving.

One does not institute an organizational management-by-objective system very quickly. In our own organization, we spent approximately five years before the system was really working well. The first year we introduced the idea of asking people for their goals for the next year. The second year we asked people to report about what they had done the previous year and once again to tell us their dreams for the following year. The third year we began to correlate all of the different goals and departments in one overall plan and spell out the actual expenditure needed for each goal. The fourth year we began to take a look at the cost benefit involved with each of the goals. It was not until the fifth year that we really began to see the system operate. And even now we find we need to review, refine, tailor, throw away some things that are not working, and introduce other things in their place. And since new people are continuing to come into the organization, we need to train and retrain continually.

There are various entry points that might be used to introduce the idea of the future and the need for considering God's desired plan into the workings of your organization.

Change the annual report.   The annual report is a good point of entry, since almost every organization puts out some kind of yearly survey. Usually this report is a recap of what each committee or department has done during the previous year. Typically, each subgroup within the organization is given one page or half a page within the annual report and asked to give some statement of what they have done. Many times this is accompanied by a financial statement as to how they spent the monies that have been allocated to them. At the time the next annual report is to be prepared, ask the people who are preparing it to modify it—by either giving each group twice as much space *or* asking each to use half the space they previously used.

In addition to reporting what happened last year, they make their statements of faith, their feelings about what God is going to do through them during the coming year. You might suggest that they indicate some of the steps that they believe they will need to go through to see these ideas bear fruit. Most people will not object to this approach and will go at the process with enthusiasm. In fact, they will enjoy trying to think about all the good things that God is going to do "next year."

Here is where your first practice in patience comes in. Receive the report and wait *for almost a year* to see what happens. Then ask that when they write the *next* report, they also show *how they did* against the statements of faith they made about what God was going to do with them during the current year. Again, ask them to repeat what they did a year before—make statements of faith about what they believe God will do in the coming year. Suddenly the light may begin to dawn! People will realize that they are going to be asked how they measured up against the goals they set, and the whole process of thinking about the future will begin. Notice that there was no need to mention anything about goals or even to teach people how to plan. All you did was request that people compare what they believed God was going to do with what they actually saw Him accomplish in their lives.

Expand the annual budget.   Another point of entry is the annual budget. It is surprising how many organizations, especially churches, do their budgeting without much thought to any planning. We are familiar with some churches that actually do their planning *after* they have completed their budget. What they do not see is that once they have adopted a budget, most of the planning is already done! Once you have decided how much money you are going to spend, you have decided a great deal about how much and what you are going to *do.*

Such churches do their planning by "extrapolation of the budget." They examine the last budget, comparing each budgeted item with how much was actually spent in that category. Then they extrapolate into the following year. For instance, take the item of salaries—usually the first on the list! A church may conclude that in the coming year the pastor may need an increase in salary, or an additional staff person may be needed. It budgets for this and may then look at all the other items—the expense of running the building, cost of materials and supplies, and so on—and make some assumptions, perhaps deciding: "Let's raise it ten percent."

After organizations have done this for each budget item, they typically total the proposed budget and compare it with the last year's income. At this point they go through an exercise of faith *based upon money* rather than on what it is they want to accomplish. In other words, they say to themselves, "Can we actually raise this much money?"

If the answer is no, very often they will cut back each budget item by the percent by which they think the total budget is too high. This type of budgeting is not difficult to do. It requires very little imagination and is all too prevalent. And to make matters worse, it focuses the attention of the planners on money rather than on what it is that God wants done.

What can you do to change this? At the occasion of the next budget, ask people to lay out five years of budgeting. Ask them to show the *past two years* (history), the proposed budget for the *present year,* and the suggested budgets for the *two future years* following the present budget year. It is extremely difficult to extrapolate a budget three years into the future. Consequently, when people attempt to move in their budget thinking from this year to three years in the future, they really have to do some planning. You will discover that the discussions going on as this is attempted will often uncover the need for setting clearer goals and doing some planning—and in general will motivate people toward the goals and the planning process.

Break down the ministry by objectives.   Another way to
introduce goals and planning through the budgeting
process is to ask people to break down the budget items
by overall ministries or by basic objectives. For instance,
as we indicated earlier, at World Vision we currently
have six basic objectives: reaching the unreached, enabling leadership, caring for children, emergency relief,
community development, and challenging to mission.
Our budget should *begin* by seeing what the cost of carrying out each one of these ministries is going to be.
Within a local church, this might be a breakdown by
worship, education, outreach, and congregational nurture. If the budgeting committee has not tried to budget
this way in the past, the problem of trying to divide up,
for example, the pastor's salary will immediately raise
the question as to what is being done, as opposed to what
should be done. (See our book *The Art of Management
for Christian Leaders* for some preliminary help on
budgeting.)

Start a planning committee.   Another point of entry is
the appointment of a planning committee or task force.
Perhaps this should be given a different name—because
a planning committee should *not* do the planning. (Remember: good goals and bad goals!) If one committee is
given the task of setting the goals and doing the planning
for an organization, it will be very difficult for the members of the organization to "buy into" somebody else's
goals. What, then, should a "planning" committee do? It
can—

- Analyze what appear to be the organization's present purposes and goals and present these back to the leadership.
- Gather information about the overall situation, as well as
  provide the organization with forecasts as to what apparently will happen in the area in which it is ministering.
- Discover what others are doing in the community or
  within the same field of operation.

- Package and present this information for those who are concerned with administration, in such a way that it will help them see the need for planning.
- Conduct training sessions to help others see how to do planning.
- Coordinate the efforts of all the different committees and departments at the time of the annual plan of the budget and bring these into a comprehensive whole.

But the act of instituting a committee may not alone get people thinking about the future and their need to deal with it in a prayerful and thoughtful way. To create a planning committee without having thought through some of the other entry points will be a disservice to those who were asked to work on the committee, as well as to those who are asked to help.

Ask about goals.   Another entry point is to give leadership in asking questions about goals. Without trying to educate people as to the difference between purposes and goals or the need for planning, a simple question— "What is it that we are trying to accomplish here?"—can often be used to direct people's thinking into the consequences of what they are doing. Begin to develop this style for your part of the organization. As this question is asked more often, people's attention will be turned not to the carrying out of the task but to reaching goals.

Experience Teaches

You can probably think of other entry points yourself. Remember, people learn better by watching others do something, and even more by doing it themselves. We do learn theoretical concepts by being lectured to in a classroom setting, but should remember that people are lukewarm to new ideas until they actually have some experience of them. Many times *you* can model that experience for them.

Further Reading

The Change Agent: The Strategy of Innovative Leadership by Lyle E. Schaller talks about the human side of planning from the Christian organizational viewpoint, and particularly the church's. Highly recommended for any pastor or Christian leader who wants to be an agent of change in his church.

The Human Side of Planning by David W. Ewing. (See reading list for chapter 7.)

12

An Overall Approach

And since we have gifts that differ according to the grace given to us, let each exercise them accordingly . . . .

Romans 12:6

Here is an overall outline of an approach to making the organizational cycle work in your organization. We will provide this outline and in subsequent chapters supply the details of how to carry out the process. We will list in Part III a number of different tools that you can use to execute some of the suggested steps.

In all of this, try to keep in mind that the *approach* to the process is the key factor. The exact steps you use will depend on the nature of your organization, your leadership style, and where the organization is at a particular point in time. We are not advocating a "how to" as much as we are recommending an *approach*.

Whether or not you are able to carry out this approach on your own (or need to gain the agreement of others within the organization) obviously depends upon your position within the organization. It is not necessary to convince people of the entire process in order to get it moving. You can take the first step of analyzing the present situation by asking people to gather ideas on future situations without deciding specifically what steps would have to be followed.

Analyze the Situation

Where are the people in the organization now? What are their perceived needs? What are their needs as you see them? In other words, how are the members of the organization seeing themselves and the future? Are there some who are discontented with the status quo?

Review what we have said about situation analysis. What is the history of the organization? What are its present commitments? What is its situation, its environment? What appear to be the goals and purposes of the organization?

Let the Process Develop the Goals

We are not suggesting a process to achieve *your* individual ends. Rather, we are trying to understand God's strategy and become a part of it. Remember what we said about a Christian organization's assumed ability to move from within as well as from without. Count on the fact that God is going to be at work in the organization and rely on the operation of the Holy Spirit and the wisdom of other leaders and people.

Gather Ideas for the Future

Here is where you would take your first overt action. Begin to gather ideas from as many people as possible. This can be done in sequence or all at one time. Ask questions about what people perceive to be the purpose of the organization. What do they believe are (or should be) the goals of the organization? This can be done in a very informal way. Some years ago we at World Vision passed out some sheets labeled "1980 Dream Sheet." We asked the organization's executives to put down their ideas of where they thought World Vision would and could be in 1980, at that time seven years away. We then asked them to relate their ideas to some of the things they were already doing. We were not asking them to do "planning" or "set goals," but to use their sanctified imagination.

You might have to begin with questions about the purposes of the organization. If these are not clear, you might want to ask people their ideas about the future, and then from these ideas sort out what people apparently believe are the purposes of the organization. (You and they may be surprised!) If you are reasonably clear about your purpose, especially if the organization has a statement of purpose or faith, you might want to put this at the top of the sheet and then ask people such questions as: "In light of the purpose of our organization, what are your dreams for what God might do with and through us ten years from now?"

There are a number of ways of gathering information. One of these is just to hand out a questionnaire. You don't have to push the collection of this information very strongly. Usually just asking people to turn it in within a week or two will be enough to get things going. Another way of doing this is to use a brainstorming technique during department or committee meetings. (One such method, the Slip Technique, is described in chapter 14.)

Sort Out Ideas You Receive

You will receive a wide range of ideas about the future and what the organization should be doing—big and small ones, immediate and long-range ones, important and insignificant ones. If you do not already have a clear statement of purpose(s), your first sorting should probably be aimed at identifying what these suggestions for the future say about the organization's perception of its purpose. From this you might want to write a general statement of purpose to send back for further work. This in itself may be provocative enough to get people to think more specifically about the future and their part in it. On the other hand, if you do have a statement of purpose, the first approach would be to try to relate these various ideas about the future to that purpose. You will usually come up with a series of different categories that fit your organization.

Once you have the ideas broken down by categories against the organization's purpose, look for ideas which appear to be dependent upon each other. For example, one person might suggest that five years from now he hopes that music will play a more prominent role in the local church. Another person might suggest installing a pipe organ. Obviously, the idea of a pipe organ relates to the idea of having an improved music program. To give an example from a Christian service organization, some-one might have the general idea that it needs to communicate better with its constituency. Another person might make the suggestion that an organizational magazine should be mailed to the constituency. Again, we see the relationship between these two suggestions.

Some suggestions will relate to others in *time*. In order for one suggestion to take place, another suggestion would have to precede it. Other suggestions will be related to their *dependency* upon another, as noted above. Still other suggestions will fall into categories of relative *importance*. Some of them obviously will have much more significance for the future than others.

All ideas should be boiled down into some kind of readable, comprehensive list. Edit where necessary. Below is a sample list of answers. Notice that there is a great variety of both big and small ideas.

SURVEY OF CONGREGATIONAL IDEAS

We need to care more for *people*.
We need to spend less money on ourselves and more on missionaries.
I think the Sunday-morning service is too long.
We need more expository preaching.

Let's build a gym.

Our missions conference needs to be improved.

Let's have guest cards in the pew racks.

When are we going to solve the parking problem?

Our church is growing too slowly. We need to reach out.

Our church is growing too rapidly. We need to build more fellowship.

We need a new Christian education building.

Let's get a business administrator around this place!

The pastor has been here too long.

What about a help line that people can call day or night?

The drapes in the sanctuary are a disgrace.

Let's get some up-to-date hymnals!

We need a stronger adult education program.

Our kids aren't learning anything in Sunday school.

We need more Thursday-evening socials and a new kitchen.

Let's have two services on Sunday mornings.

Let's divide the church into fellowship groups.

We need an evangelism team or committee.

We need to care for our missionaries better when they're home.

Let's publish a book of the pastor's sermons. They're great!

The lighting in the sanctuary is terrible. I can hardly see the hymns.

When are we going to get out of the local council?

Our church bulletin board needs a new coat of paint.

Let's build a new sanctuary that really glorifies God!

There's dust on the back of the pews.

Next we have arranged these by what appear to be general categories. Some obviously can be placed in more than one category. As we look at our items, we see both comments on the situation as it exists now and suggestions as to how it might be improved. We can learn a great deal by both what is said and what is *not* said. For example, there are no suggestions about the physical needs of the local community. There seems to be a general emphasis on things that other people should be doing, rather than the people who made the suggestions.

IDEAS ARRANGED BY CATEGORY

Outreach to the Community

Let's have guest cards in the pew racks.
When are we going to solve our parking problem?
Our church is growing too slowly. We need to reach out.
What about a help line that people can call day or night?
Let's have two services on Sunday mornings.
We need an evangelism team or committee.
Our church bulletin board needs a new coat of paint.

Outreach to the World

We need to spend less money on ourselves and more on missionaries.
Our missions conference needs to be improved.
We need to care for our missionaries better when they're home.

Christian Nurture

Let's build a gym.
We need to care more for *people*.
We need more expository preaching.
We need a new Christian education building.
We need a stronger adult education program.
Our kids aren't learning anything in Sunday school.
We need more Thursday-evening socials and a new kitchen.
Our church is growing too rapidly. We need more fellowship.
I think the Sunday-morning service is too long.
The drapes in the sanctuary are a disgrace.
Let's get some up-to-date hymnals.
Let's have two services on Sunday mornings.
Let's publish a book of the pastor's sermons. They're great!
The lighting in the sanctuary is terrible. I can hardly see the hymns.

Let's build a new sanctuary that really glorifies God.
There's dust on the back of the pews.

Miscellaneous

Let's get a business administrator around this place!
The pastor has been here too long.
When are we going to get out of the local council?

Notice that you have already begun to get people involved with the process. We all like to be asked our opinion about things. It is fun to speculate on the future, particularly when we do not have a sense of having to be personally involved in our speculations. By asking people about the future, you will raise their consciousness about it. There is a point to be made here about the power of a survey or questionnaire. The very act of taking the survey immediately raises questions about the reasons for the survey and its implications. Surveys are never neutral. They always upset or change in some way the group which is being surveyed. (For more information about surveys see *How Can I Get Them to Listen?* by James F. Engel.)

Give Feedback

You now need to find some way to keep people informed as to what they have been saying and what others have been saying. This can be done in many ways. For Christian organizations, one way is to have a staff meeting and have someone summarize what has been said. In the local church you might want to have a congregational meeting and/or publish some kind of report. Just giving back to the congregation the list of ideas they submitted, as shown in our example, would tell them a great deal about what other people are thinking and would begin to generate new ideas in different individuals. In any event, it is important that people have some feedback soon after giving their input. Otherwise they may forget what they said. So keep the process moving. Keep people thinking about what is happening. If you have actually had approval to begin a formal process, in the case of a local church you may want to give this feedback in a series of meetings that are open to the entire congregation. In an organization a report to the appropriate people on the executive staff is in order. In other words, make *long-range* work out of long-range planning by deciding ahead of time that you will meet on a monthly basis to review what has been said so far and to report back to the group. In the case of a local church, even though everyone may not come to a congregational meeting, the fact that all have had the opportunity to come will mean a great deal to them. Note what we said about the need for the congregation to have veto power. In all of this keep reminding people that you are feeding back to them a summary of their own ideas.

Ask for Goals

Assuming that you are able to write an overall statement of purpose (or such a statement exists), go back to the committees, task forces, or functional units within the organization and ask each to state five goals they have for the coming year (for each purpose to which they relate)—and five goals for the year after that. You do not have to explain to them the difference between goals and purposes. If you take the next step of asking them also to list five *steps* for each goal, many times they will give you five purposes with five (measurable and accomplishable) goals to go with them.

Most people will not resist this approach. After all, you have not stated that you are going to hold them accountable for their goals. You are just trying to get an overview of what is going on. The answers that you receive from your initial data gathering will do much to help the committees or departments think about their goals.

Arrange Goals by Purposes

Now that each functional unit has submitted some goals, the time has come to see whether goals actually support the purposes of the organization. In Figure 14 we have illustrated this in a simple chart. In the left-

GROUP NAME	ORGANIZATION PURPOSE			

Figure 14

hand column we suggest that you list the group name of the committee, task force, department, or whatever is your organizational unit. Under "Organization Purpose" list the apparent major purposes of your organization. (If you have six major purposes, the chart will obviously have to be six spaces wide.)

Now take the goals that each group has given you and, using some identification such as a simple 1-2-3 numbering system, locate each group's goals under a specific purpose. You may need an empty column at the end for goals that do not appear to relate to any purpose.

This will present you with an immediate picture of where there are missing goals or steps to support a purpose—or where there are a number of goals that apparently have nothing to do with the purposes of the organization. At this point you have a fairly compact picture of what the organization believes are its purposes as compared to what it says it is trying to accomplish through its goals.

Again, feed this back to everyone concerned, so that all can have a picture of what is going on. Do not expect people to get tremendously enthusiastic about this yet. Some will just view it as an exercise. We will begin to identify some goal owners in the next step.

Hold a Planning Retreat or Conference

The purpose of a planning retreat or conference can be threefold: (1) to rank by priority ("prioritize") various goals in terms of purpose; (2) to make some general plans to meet these goals; and (3) to identify goal owners through the process of planning.

The need for preparation.   We have dedicated a chapter in Part III to the subject of holding a planning conference. The significant thing to note here is that some *preparation is needed.* In the case of a local church, it is useful to invite and encourage every member of the congregation to come. Except in the case of a very small church, the entire congregation might not come, but the important thing is that they are all invited. Advertise well in advance. How important it seems to you will be an indication as to how important it appears to the rest of the people. In a day in which our senses are continually bombarded by advertising from many different forms of media, we subconsciously equate the number of times a message is repeated with how important it is. How far in advance it is announced is also important. Everyone knows that important events are recognized long before they happen!

You have to prepare an "experience" that members will enjoy and which will also be a learning time. We suggest that the planning conference be held away from the church (or headquarters of the organization) in a "neutral" territory. You will need a facility that is large enough to handle all of the different things that you will want to go through. Very often just going to the building or offices of a sister organization is enough to get people away from their usual environment (and especially from their telephones).

People will have to be trained to be leaders of a planning conference. Plan for this. Here is where a planning committee is very useful. If its members are qualified, they can carry out this function. Qualifications are not so much planning skills as they are skills in group dynamics. Needed are people who are good facilitators and enablers, rather than people who are directive in their leadership approach. It is important that everyone understands the purposes of the planning conference and what the outcomes are supposed to be, and that each personally feels accepting of the approaches to be used.

Evaluating goals. Begin with a list of all the goals organized under the different purposes of the organization. You may have to do some prior editing of this list to break it down into manageable size, but it is important to get people involved in prioritizing the goals. In chapter 17 we have given a sample rating sheet that we used in our own church's planning conference. From this you can develop your own priority or evaluation form. Note that one of the places to exercise leadership is the assigning of values or weight to the various questions listed.

You can use the ABC Technique described in chapter 15 to obtain people's consensus about the value of each goal.

Let us assume, for instance, that you have a planning conference with a hundred people present, that they are divided into ten groups of ten people, and that you have a hundred goals to evaluate. You might give each group ten goals and ask members to prioritize these goals. After they have done so, they may have time to do some planning on the goal(s) with the highest priority. This process of discussing each goal in terms of a series of prioritizing questions will in itself prepare people for a great deal of the work needed to plan the ones that they have chosen. As people verbalize their own ideas about particular goals, it helps them to clarify their feelings and to develop their own internal priorities based upon their value system. This business of selecting the most important goals is therefore a good beginning for the planning process.

After the groups have gone through the prioritizing procedure, take them through a planning exercise on at least one goal. There is a wide variety of techniques that you can use here. Remember that group planning needs to be clearly divided into data gathering, idea evaluation, and idea synthesis into an overall plan. The major difficulty encountered in group planning is in the tendency for some people to come to immediate conclusions before everyone has contributed input on the data. This is why the Slip Technique, a variation of brainstorming, is so useful. (See chapter 14.)

Decide ahead of time how people are going to *display* their plans to one another. We like the PERT Technique described in chapter 15. It seems overly complicated to some people, and (for those who have used it in industry) may bring back too many strong memories of schedules they *had* to keep. But it does give people a way of displaying what they have done and provides them with a sense of accomplishment.

While the group sessions on both prioritizing and planning are going on, seek to *identify potential goal owners*—people who are particularly positive and vocal about a particular goal. Many times people become so enthusiastic that they almost demand that they be given the responsibility to carry out the goal. They are really motivated to see something happen! Remember that all people are motivated, and leaders have to discover what motivates them. They are not just motivated by the things by which *we* would like them to be motivated, but by varying situations and circumstances. It is not our task to say, "How can I motivate them?" We can find out what already motivates them by taking the people through a planning process which allows them to identify with a particular plan. One can assume that if a particular goal was deemed to have the highest priority by a small group and the plans were then made to execute this goal, there would be at least one or two people who would be already motivated towards reaching that goal. These are the people whom we want to have as goal owners.

Reporting to the whole. Leave time at the end of the planning session for members of each group to report to the whole about which of their goals they thought had the highest priority—and which ones they actually planned in some detail. Here is where the display will be very useful. This reporting will not only cement their own feelings about what they have done, but it will begin to induce a sense of goal ownership. When people get involved in reporting on plans that they have put together, they begin to identify with them.

Feedback. After a planning retreat, it is again necessary to feed back the overall results to everyone concerned. We need to remind ourselves repeatedly that not everyone will read such a report (and that even fewer may be really excited about it). But the absence of such a report will work against people's future involvement, while the presence of such a report indicates that *somebody* is doing *something*.

Resolve Conflicts

It would be extremely unusual if all of the goals and purposes worked on at the planning conference neatly fit together. Life is not that simple. There will be conflicts, because we cannot do everything at the same time or because one goal will be vying for attention and resources with another. There will even be conflicts because some goals or purposes are actually contradictory to each another. And conflict in goals probably means conflict in people.

Conflict is healthy. Or to put it another way, *healthy* conflict is good. If there were no differences of opinion about the way the world is or might be, how dull life would be. When people are open and able to state what they believe without fear of being denigrated, healthy conflict is possible. It is too bad that we cannot come up with a better word for it. But more and more people are recognizing that "conflict management" or creative tension is a very useful tool. By allowing people an environment in which they can state their opinions and beliefs, we allow them to ventilate a great deal of feeling. (See reading list: *Increasing Leadership Effectiveness.*) As you use the Slip Technique, you will discover that this is one way for people to state opposing views and get them down on paper. We need to get differences of opinion out in the open. Once we know that we have been heard, we are usually ready to move on to compromise.

"Compromise" is another word that carries too much negative freight. Practically all of life is a compromise. If you don't like "compromise," perhaps "resolution" would sound better. But the fact remains that I may have to modify *my* goals in order to be able to work on *your* goals—and still achieve *my* goals.

Conflict is best managed by analyzing whether it is possible to do all the things we want within the allowable time frame. There may be three or four major programs competing for attention. Although we may not be able to do them all this year, this does not mean that some must be discarded. If we schedule them over a period of three years, we not only give everyone the feeling that eventually we will do them, but we give ourselves a great deal more time to plan for them. Meanwhile, those who are enthusiastic, potential goal owners can be involved in the planning and refining process to ensure that the goal will be worked on and carried out with the very best thinking and the greatest amount of possible prayer. Indeed, it would be very good if we could turn the tables around and have people vying for which goal would come *third*, rather than first, just so adequate planning and prayer might be provided.

Some of the techniques we described in chapter 7 for the planning conference can also be used for conflict resolution by holding smaller conferences. By dividing people into groups and asking them to discuss the pros and cons of seemingly opposite positions and then reporting back to the larger group, much can be done to find good conflict resolution. We can also make people feel as though they have been part of the resolution process. Again, we cannot overemphasize how important this is.

We probably need to have an aside here to call attention to the fact that God *will* get His work done. He calls upon us to attempt to uncover His strategy and become part of it. It is a very releasing concept to know that in every day there are always enough hours to do the perfect will of God.

Assign Responsibility

If several goal owners have been identified, the task of assigning responsibility is already under way. But a goal only becomes operational and workable when there are goal owners available. Responsibility may be assigned because relevant committees or departments already exist, or because a special task force is being formed. The important thing is that there is a name attached and a feeling of ownership for every goal.

Complete the Planning

It is obvious that you cannot do a whole year's planning in one day and that the specific groups that are going to be involved in the planning need detailed assignments of responsibility. In fact, as the organization begins to adopt the concept of a yearly planning cycle, planning retreats can be used increasingly to deal with the long-range future rather than with goals of the coming year. The various subgroups will begin to fit naturally into doing the planning and their own thinking. This is highly desirable. If the goals have been assigned to the right committee or department, this is obviously the place to build goal ownership.

It may be that a period of weeks or months will be required before the individual committees can get their detailed planning completed and in turn can submit their budget requirements, human resource needs, and schedules to the overall organization for integration into the total program. *Plan* to take your time.

Set Schedules

This may have already been done within the plan. However, make sure that all of the plans have schedules which have been reviewed one against another for possible conflicts and overlap. When setting schedules, make sure from a management viewpoint that you build in times of review and evaluation of progress. Schedules have to be owned in the same way that goals have to be owned. You cannot arbitrarily assign schedules. The best way is for people to work out their schedules jointly.

Provide Resources

Resources may have already been contemplated and built into the planning. However, before they can be allocated, we have to make sure that they are available. We have to add up all of the required resources from each of the plans to make sure the total needed is available. This may seem obvious, but it is surprising how many times people come up with good ideas for which they do not have the necessary energy or finances. As with schedules, we have to see that there is no overlap. Do not forget that resources do not include only money and facilities. Our major resource is the *people* who are going to do the work. Make a clear estimate of the hours that are going to be involved in carrying out each of the goals and make certain that, when you add up all of those hours, they do not exceed the number of hours available within the organization! Remember that "a day's work" is seldom accomplished in a day.

Too often, local churches unthinkingly pile program on program, expecting that the laity is going to be able to fit into each one. The assumption seems to be that every lay person is gifted for every task. When the entire congregation is challenged to carry out a new task, there are bound to be those who are not able to meet that challenge. The challenge will leave them feeling guilty. Others will feel dissatisfied that not everybody is "cooperating." Be careful with human resources—our most precious assets!

Go Into Action

Obviously, the work on different goals starts at different times, but there is a natural tendency for us to plan in blocks of a year. We think of the next fiscal year as the time when we actually begin work on goals and perhaps complete them. It may not work that way; we will run into problems. Leadership is necessary for managing plans and people. Correction and evaluation will be needed. Someone who understands the organizational cycle needs to maintain an overview of the organization, both to encourage and redirect it toward its goals.

Review and Evaluate Regularly

The way to make sure that we stay on course, or take a new course if this is indicated, is to make certain that we have scheduled points of review. There will be some goal owners who lose their enthusiasm as they run into troubled waters. There may be new leaders who emerge, as well as a need to postpone some goals in order to work further on others.

Don't get trapped into thinking of planning as rigid steps which need to be followed dogmatically. Plans are our attempt both to anticipate what the future will be like and to have an impact on that future. For the Christian, they are an attempt to align our purposes with God's. "It is pleasant to see plans develop. That is why fools refuse to give them up even when they are wrong" (Proverbs 13:19 LB).

Repeat Each Year

We do not mean by the above that we do exactly the same thing in the coming year that we did in the last. Rather, in some formal way we should go through this *process* each year. The business of evaluating our purposes and our former goals and of setting new goals and thinking about plans for them is the juice that keeps us alive and moving. Why each year? There is nothing particularly important about doing it on a yearly basis, except that our society thinks and operates that way. Most organizations naturally fall into the yearly season that is our Christian heritage.

In Figure 15 at the end of this chapter, we have reproduced a chart that has been adapted from an article by Speed Leas entitled "Management by Objectives in the Church." This chart has obviously been worked out for a church with a congregational form of government and/or a ruling board. The process starts at the top, with the official board's development of a list of goals and committees to implement them, which results in a written list of goals with committee assignments. Review, implementation, and evaluation follow. Notice that point number nine is a repeat of point number one. On the facing page (155) we have taken the liberty of rearranging this into a circle (Figure 16). This cycle fits any organization and can be adapted to individual requirements.

Further Reading

Effective Management by Objectives: The 3-D Method of MBO by W. J. Reddin is a very readable discussion of MBO. Reddin does a good job of spelling out what "management by objective" is and how to implement an MBO program within the organization. He also points out some of the dangers.

The Decision-Makers: How to Improve the Quality of Decision-Making in the Churches by Lyle E. Schaller is another of Schaller's contributions to the growing body of literature on the application of the management theory in a Christian context.

Joining Together: Group Theory and Group Skills by David W. Johnson and Frank P. Johnson is an excellent workbook on group theory and group skills. Particularly helpful in understanding the dynamics of group decision making, goal setting, leadership, communication, problem solving. Contains a number of skill-training exercises. An excellent book for anyone involved in leading a group within an organization (or with a nonorganizational setup).

Group Processes: An Introduction to Group Dynamics is Joseph Luft's introduction to the dynamics of group activity. A good book for someone who wants to get a more technical understanding of group processes, including such concepts as the Johari Window, interaction patterns, metacommunications, as well as organizational behavior.

Meeting Yourself Halfway by Sidney B. Simon has over thirty value-clarification strategies for daily living. Very helpful for the individual as well as for groups.

Increasing Leadership Effectiveness by Chris Argyris is an actual case study of what happened when six company presidents worked over a period of years to allow healthy conflict and confrontation in their organizations.

Books on Day-to-Day Management

Tools for Time Management by Edward R. Dayton is a "toolbox" of both techniques and principles for more effective time management. The book is arranged in alphabetical form, so that the reader can either follow through the complete logic or dip in wherever he pleases.

The Time Trap: Managing Your Way Out by Alex MacKenzie begins with the problem of managing yourself as a key to managing your time. Has an excellent section on working with your secretary.

How to Get Control of Your Time and Your Life by Alan Lakein is just about what it says. It approaches time management (as does *Tools for Time Management* above) from the viewpoint of first establishing the *personal* goals and then moving on to what you need to do next to realize them.

A Strategy for Daily Living by Ari Kiev is a small book that does what few books do: It makes its point and then stops. The point is that goals are very powerful motivators and that identifying and pursuing personal goals is an effective strategy for daily living.

WORK PLAN

WHO	WHAT	Sept.	Oct.	Nov.	Dec.	Jan.	Feb.	Mar.	Apr.	May	June	July	Aug.	RESULTS
(1) Official Board	Develops list of goals and committees to implement them													Written list of goals with committee assignments
(2) Total Congregation	Meets to review and modify goals													Goals and assignments ratified
(3) Each Committee	Reviews its goals & writes specific objectives for the year													Written objectives
(4) Official Board with each Committee	Reviews & approves each committee's objectives													Written approval
(5) Each Committee	Implements objectives													Achieved objectives
(6) Each Committee	Evaluates its performance against objectives													Written evaluation
(7) Official Board	Reviews each committee's performance													Written evaluation
(8) Board & Committee	Shares evaluation with each committee													Feedback session with each committee
(9) Official Board	Develops list of goals & committees to implement them													Written list of goals with committee assignments

Adapted from "Management by Objectives in the Church" by Speed Leas (The Christian Ministry, Nov. 1973, p. 11), with permission.

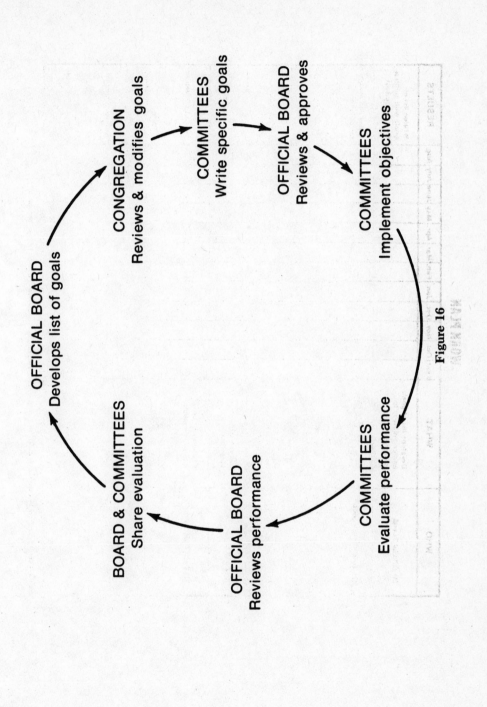

Figure 16

13

A Case Study

The following article—"Solving the Problems: Planning" by Gerald P. Foster, Ph.D.—originally appeared in *Theology, News and Notes* (October 1973) and is used by permission of the author.

The official board of Faith Church was assembled in the church conference room. The occasion was a special meeting of the board to listen to Sam Baxter's ideas on church planning. Sam Baxter, owner of Baxter Enterprises, a growing business firm in the area, was a new member of Faith Church. Everyone was getting to know Sam through his comments on appropriate occasions. "We need to be more businesslike around here!" was a recurrent theme. His latest concerns had been the church's lack of long-range planning. The board had agreed to hear him out.

*　　*　　*

"Gentlemen, modern business today must plan, and plan carefully and comprehensively, if it is to survive. No longer is it possible to be successful in business operating on a day-to-day basis, to be content with the status quo. A look to the future—the immediate future, the long-range future—is required. Goals must be made clear, priorities must be set and operating plans designed. In successful firms, plans are laid for the next period, the next year, the next five years. Twenty years ahead is not an inappropriate period to consider of concern.

157

"When you plan, people are caught up into the future, not shocked and confused by it; serious mistakes are avoided, false starts are minimized or eliminated, the purposes and objectives of the enterprise are better achieved. When you know what you are doing, where you are going and how you propose to get there—specifically, chronologically and in measurable ways—confidence is generated. Opportunities are easier to see, problems are more easily defined. Somehow, they become easier to handle. Modern business is a complex matter in this era of rapid and constant change and ferment, and plans are vital tools, essential to have in dealing with that complexity. Plans can be useful to Faith Church.

"Plans form a firm basis for the allocation and control of scarce resources. They help with describing and delegating the essential tasks to be performed. They assist us in deciding when and how these tasks should be performed if established goals are to be met, and in what order. Plans are a key to effective and efficient performance.

"Plans are expensive. They take time and effort to prepare. They cost money. But plans properly prepared produce predictable results. And that to a businessman is important!

"I am convinced Faith Church, just as my business, can pinpoint what it wishes to accomplish and accomplish it through careful planning. I know the value of planning. I see its tangible effects in the profits my business earns. The church, Faith Church, can learn of its value as well.

"I mentioned the need to know what we are about at Faith. Where we are going! This, I propose, is where we start in our planning effort here. First, establish our targets! What do we want to accomplish? What do we want to bring about? What do we want our future to be?

When we have the answers to these questions before us, in clear and measurable terms, the future becomes a visible reality, a reality to live with. Under such circumstances, the future takes on a momentum of its own, carrying us along through the rough spots with the smooth.

"When the future is clear, specific measurable goals can be stated and classified as to scope and priority. Tasks can be related to the ends in view in a logical sequence. Sequences of events and activities can be synchronized. An efficient and realistic pattern of concerted, coordinated and connected action can be derived. Such a result is guaranteed to produce the desired end.

"With the pattern of tasks, goals and priorities clear, we can calculate the resources we need. The requirements of the plan for men, money, materials, methods, facilities and time can be computed. How will we meet these needs and requirements? What kind of a pace should we set? People like clear challenges. They get discouraged if the pace is too overwhelming but they soon get bored if it is not demanding enough.

"With our plan ready for implementation, control becomes most important. Research on operations and the feedback and forward of information on activities becomes vital. We must be able to continuously monitor the degree of conformance of results with plans. Intermediate stages of progress thus are defined, and milestones are established as check-points along the way to keep us on the track. What do we need to know now to insure future activity conforming to plan and priority? How do we identify problems and false directions before they defeat us? How do we measure movement toward the objective we seek early enough to exploit opportunities, and clearly enough to complete action incisively, to gain that thrill of reaching our goal? When, then, do we regroup and replan? The answers to these

questions can only come from an adequate information
system established as an integral part of the overall plan.

"Perhaps, despite our best efforts, our initial plans
prove unsatisfactory. Should this occur, we are in a
realistic position, having planned carefully, to replan.
The plan itself, and what we now know about its
deficiencies, becomes a superior opportunity to produce
a better result. Thus, experience becomes cumulative.
Our image of the future is refined through use and reflection. We retain our vision, and we have the means of
maintaining it and keeping it under control.

"May I suggest we plan our future this way here in
Faith Church. Let's decide together where we want to
be in five years. Let's clarify and identify the problems
and opportunities we see; then get the facts, analyze
them carefully and develop alternative approaches to
moving ahead. The risks, costs and benefits of each alternative can then be calculated. Implementation of our
best choice can then follow.

"President Kennedy frequently told the story of a
French marshal who asked his gardener one day to plant
a tree. The gardener protested, 'It will take a hundred
years to grow!' 'In that case, we have no time to lose,' the
marshal responded. 'Plant it now!'

"Gentlemen, we have no time to lose here! Now is the
time for us to plan."

*   *   *

"What did you think of Sam Baxter's talk last night,
Pastor?" Bill Rogers, Faith's senior layman was on the
phone. Faith Church's pastor, Richard McVey, had ta' 'n
the call at home.

"Sam was certainly enthusiastic and persuasive, Bill.
What he said was all very logical, and I think I can see
how it would work well for Sam, but I'm not at all sure
we can do things just that way in Faith Church."

"Oh? Why is that, Pastor?"

"I haven't thought it through really, Bill, but I can't help but feel that something is missing in what Sam proposes. For me, at least, the essence of the Church and its mission doesn't seem to come through the verbiage. I guess I expect church planning to be different somehow."

I suspect that many pastors, like Dick McVey, would be somewhat uneasy about Sam Baxter's recommendations. I would guess that many of you reading this article have sat through similar presentations by well-meaning laymen, and echo Pastor McVey's concerns.

Such concerns are perhaps well taken! Planning for commercial ventures is necessarily cold-blooded and task-centered. Factors vital to church functioning are likely to be neglected when such single-valued approaches are employed. In addition, our experience with church planning is limited, and so far has been inconclusive at best as to its proper configuration or its real value. Faith Church is not a business and probably cannot be run successfully as one. The situation, I suggest, is much more complex.

Planning in the Church

In an earlier article we suggested an ordering of priorities quite different from the results-oriented priorities of Sam Baxter's proposal. We suggested we start with our relationships, first our relationship with God. Second, our relationships with each other as members of the Body of Christ. Both relationships were viewed as of higher priority than our task. If these are the proper priorities for the Christian, they properly should be reflected in procedures for church planning as well.

"It was Augustine and then Calvin who used the concept of alienation to emphasize that the problem of sin or evil was not just theological but *relational*—a breach of man's relationship with God entailing a breach of all other relationships. The alienation of evil is theological, between God and man; sociological, between man and other men; psychological, between man and himself; and ecological, between man and nature." [1]

The business milieu reflects to a substantial degree all of these alienations. It would be the height of irony if the church at this juncture in its history should begin to express its essence and its mission among men as an echo of business experience.

Also, it is well to keep a proper perspective with respect to the present state of the art of church planning. Our capacity to "invent the future" is increasing rapidly. However, the expansion of that capacity beyond the scope of present experience may be premature. The knowledge, skills and attitudes essential to success in planning are not broadly held by church professionals. There seem to be sufficient differences between the church and other forms of organization to counsel caution with respect to untested technological transfer. There are several reasons for this:

1. The church is not an economic institution. It is not a social or exclusively human institution. Transcendental values are very much involved. The church's role and mission in society is quite different from that of the business firm operating in a market where economic performance is primary and utility is measured by profit.

2. Business firms are staffed with "employees," churches depend heavily on "volunteers." Unlike employees whose motivations and management are cast largely in economic symbols, volunteers subsist on a psychological "income" largely social in its derivation. As Newton Malony has pointed out . . . "There is a direct relationship between overall general morale in a church and the number of leadership roles provided for its members," and pastors are advised by Malony against oversimplifying organizational and administrative ar-

rangements. "The more complex the division of labor, the better!" [2]

3. The economic enterprise in our society can safely ignore its social and religious responsibilities. It can suppress people and eternity. The Church by its very nature cannot.

4. Planning, to some, is intruding on God's exclusive territory. Edward T. Hall, in his classic, *The Silent Language,* tells of the Arab farmer, in an encounter with an American on a technical assistance mission, who expressed high indignation and anger when suggestions were made designed to improve his crop yields in the future; to influence the future was for the Arab farmer an "intrusion on the province of God." When proposing planning concepts to pastors and church professionals, some hearers have voiced similar reservations.

5. In the Church, spontaneity may be more highly valued than certainty of result.

Planning As Technology

The emerging capacity of man to influence his future, to actively plan, is what Sam Baxter is interested in. Our interest here is in the technology and the ethics of planning under church auspices. Will man's planned activity in redeeming God's creation be harmonious or discordant, functional or dysfunctional, with "that moving strength at the heart of events, straining for future fulfillment," which is God? [3] If man has no role in it, it would seem presumptuous and foolish for the church to plan. If God has no role in the events and activities under consideration, the entity involved in planning, whatever its designation, clearly is not the church. If God and man are "to fill the earth and subdue it" as we are counseled to do in Genesis, our joint venture with God becomes a technological as well as a theological project, and the influencing of the future becomes an ethical exercise. [4]

The implications of such a view of man's role and purpose in joint venture with the Creator of the universe are indeed sobering. If we are so to function, it must be as worthy craftsmen, in his image. His plan is a perfect plan, his gifts are perfect gifts, the nature of which is no less than that fully documented in the Scriptures and ideally exemplified for us in the person and work of Jesus Christ. As co-workers we must discover God's plan and implement it responsibly as befits our status. High standards of respect for the redeemed dictates a high valuation of individuals as a meta-measure of our responsiveness to divine purposes and objectives and of our responsibility in planning and problem-solving in the Church.

The view of the Church in the world proposed here has little in common with other enterprises. The Body of Christ becomes a divine institution fully equipped by God unto all good works. Its goals are accomplished through his gifts, uniquely and fully given to each of us according to our place. Each individual's place is established for him by God as efficacious and essential to the achievement of the total mission of his Church.

Against a backdrop of the Church as a joint venture with God, then, can a plan of man's become a valid image of the future, profitable for energizing the Church? If it takes into account, in inventing the future, God's transcendent interests and the unique freedoms which accrue to man therefrom—if man's role in it is to serve as a collaborator with the original author—despite basic differences between the circumstances of administration in the Church and the circumstances of administration in other milieu, it would seem it can.

God's Plan As Premise

The Scriptures are not a text on planning, but they do contain God's plan. They also contain the divine charter of the Church. Good practice would suggest planning and problem-solving start here. "We know that all that happens to us is working for our good, if we love God and if we are fitting into his plans." [5] Both the Old and the New Testament attest to this plan God has for his world. They also testify to the role that we have, individually and collectively, in carrying it forward. If the Church is different as an organized entity subject to different administrative principles and procedures, and I have suggested this is the case, its uniqueness stems from its unique charter and role. This is no small advantage. God promises us a degree of harmony "which passeth understanding" when his plan is honored. The "very stones may cry out" against us if we do not.

Secular organizations are not constrained by a prescribed relationship with God. Predominantly, self-interest is highly valued and "Love thy neighbor" turns to "Shove thy neighbor" when self dominates. Secular enterprise, as the very name implies, centers on man and his works. The plans Sam Baxter cites as the key to the success of his growing business are properly focused on Sam's aspirations and expectations, his employees are not free to question them in our concept of the corporation. The dependencies and subordinations correctly assumed by Sam Baxter in his planning are not the interdependencies and autonomies we must assume as normative characteristics of the community of the redeemed. The church in its administrative and planning processes must use different assumptions and values, it must pay attention not only to God's premises, but to God's promises to every man who believes.

Representativeness As a Requisite

Fortunately, planning and problem-solving procedures need not necessarily imply subordination, nor devaluation and abridgement of individual choice. Church planning must be carefully done not to imply either. Planning and problem-solving as we envision it means the exercise of choice in the present from among a rich set of available futures. Procedures can become irrelevant to our real needs when such choices are made for us—especially in the church!

* * *

"How do we find out what our people really want, what their real needs are?" Bill Rogers was having lunch with Pastor McVey.

"I've been giving this much thought, Bill," the Pastor responded. "I don't remember Sam saying much on this point, but it seems to me planning the future for Faith Church five years ahead has implications which dictate a high degree of consensus. Fixing the future circumscribes the options of our people. I would say we must make absolutely sure everyone affected by the plan is in agreement with it."

"You are talking about a high standard of agreement, Pastor. We have been content with less."

Faith Church Plans Its Future

Press Release (Date line Jan. 23, 1979) [6]

On January 23, 1974, Faith Church launched a five-year program of activities, the impact of which was celebrated in a congregational meeting today.

The Reverend Richard McVey, Faith Church's pastor, officiated at the special services. Pastor McVey is in his 9th year of ministry at Faith Church and under his leadership the church has shown new character and concerns both as a congregation and as a corporate citizen of the surrounding community. Many of the plans and programs envisoned only five years ago have come to pass. The new life in Faith Church is felt abroad in the area, as the friendliness and concern of its members spreads. A new spiritual emphasis at the neighborhood level has done much to unite the church.

In 1973, a lay leadership determined to "involve everyone" in the work of forward planning made Faith Church an exciting place. Reforms were instituted to insure responsiveness to grass-roots needs. Under the leadership of a Planning Committee, a series of meetings were held. The first was a well-publicized "kick-off" family pot luck supper. The program that evening was designed to maximize representation of all elements of the church in the planning process to come. A second meeting, an all-day event, was held to deal with the details. Similar meetings are now a yearly feature of life at Faith Church.

The establishment of "neighborhoods" in 1974 has been the key to a new closeness and evangelical outreach for the church in its community. Cross cutting the neighborhoods has been a small group movement centered on uniting people with similar interests regardless of geographical location. The six couples who undertook the original effort in 1974 were successful in spawning a dozen such groups still active today.

A Resources Assessment Program (RAP) instituted in the spring of 1974 continues to inventory the resources of talent and unique gifts among Faith's members. Skills matched with needs by the program have resulted in improved utilization of volunteers and in increased personal motivation to serve.

Pastor McVey, aware of the congregation's growing interest in evangelism after Key '73, the nationwide program of coordinated evangelism, has been successful in raising the level of effort even above the levels achieved in that year.

As a result of the new life in Faith Church, membership has risen in numbers and commitment. The church staff has been increased. A new vision of missions is also evident. In reflecting on the past years, Pastor McVey attributes much of the progress to the 1973 decision to plan Faith's future.

"Our board chairman, Sam Baxter, convinced us of the need for planning, bringing to us an expertise based on his experiences as president of Baxter Enterprises. We learned together how to adapt what was known about planning in business to the special requirements of Faith Church. Over the years we have remained faithful to two principles: our planning must reflect God's plan, and that plan is broadly shared with the community and the congregation. Prayer, petition, study of the Scriptures and publication of the results of our discussions are our constant planning companions. We view what we do here as a joint venture, and we are careful in all that we do to keep ourselves open to the ministry of others—and to God."

Conclusion

The case for church planning and the justification for man's efforts in the resolution of problems in the church and in society, lies in a view of man's role as co-worker with God in redeeming and subduing the world. Our growing capacity to invent the future, when employed as an expression of our high calling, can be a blessing. When informed with God's high purposes and pursued within the context of our Christian freedoms, it can contribute to our enjoyment of God. As an expression and instrument of our self-sufficiency and independence of God, it can be a curse.

A scenario such as the above for Faith Church may leave much to be desired in meeting the standard for church planning set forth here. The mere creation of the document and its broad dissemination in the church community, however, can lead to a healthy anticipatory fulfillment of its visions. Because it's there, its refinement and self-correction is enhanced. Not unlike the balancing of a broom on its handle, inverted on your palm—it's a simple task if you keep your eyes on the broom head above, impossible if you watch your hand— the future embodied in a plan assures its own fulfillment. If, looking to the future, man "discovers God's plan" as the ground of his own collaboration, his success is assured.

Source Notes

1. Os Guiness, *The Dust of Death*, Downer's Grove, Ill. InterVarsity Press, 1973. Pages 35–6 (Emphasis is mine).

2. H. Newton Malony, "Motivation and Management," *Theology: News and Notes* Volume XVIII No. 4 (Dec.) 1972. Page 18.

3. I am indebted to Kenneth Vaux, a student of the theological humanism of Helmut Thieleke, for the theology of cybernation and planning basic to this analysis. See Kenneth Vaux, *Subduing the Cosmos: Cybernetics and Man's Future*, Richmond, Va. John Knox Press, 1970.

4. *Ibid.*

5. Kenneth Taylor, *The Living Bible*, Romans 8:28.

6. The forward-dated "Press Release" is one way of documenting a plan. Scenarios such as this make living with the plan in anticipation of its fulfillment a feasible procedure. Well done and distributed, it incorporates the attributes of a self-fulfilling prophesy, a charter of assurance and hope, a presence effective in accomplishing an agreed future state.

Part III

Methods and Tools

14 Group Planning Techniques
15 Planning Tools
16 Meetings
17 The Planning Conference

14

Group Planning Techniques

. . . let us consider how to stimulate one another to love and good deeds, not forsaking our own assembling together, as is the habit of some, but encouraging one another . . . .

Hebrews 10:24, 25

In the previous section we discussed overall procedures for moving the organization ahead through the group process. We have suggested that the way to do this is to have goals which are jointly developed by as many people as possible and plans in which everyone feels a part. In the following chapters, we will get to some of the "how to."

Group Relations

There was a time when common wisdom said that great ideas and inventions came only from individuals. If that was ever true, it is no longer so. Despite all of the jokes about committees, it is through joint endeavor that human progress is made in the Western World. This means that we must find some ways to bring people together to do corporate thinking, inventing, uncovering the future, or whatever term we might use to describe planning—the process of trying to find ways of reaching a given goal.

Corporate or group planning cannot be done by just any admixture of people. Certain characteristics and affinities are needed. There must be a shared assumption about the present situation in which the organization finds itself and the future it faces. The people involved in the group planning process will be able to work together to the degree that they hold a common view. On the other side is the fact that if a group is *too* homogeneous, there is a danger of its becoming ingrown and coming up with the same old solutions, even though the problems have changed. Irving L. Janis, in his book *Victims of Groupthink*, points out that when a group is too cohesive, or too willing to bow to the whims of its leadership, it can often make very poor decisions. What is needed is "a member of the loyal opposition" to keep the group in line.

In the "paid staff" situation, individuals will spend many hours together over a period of time, interacting on the telephone and through memos, generally coming to know one another. As time passes, respect (or lack of it) will be built up. It becomes possible for someone normally to take a different or opposing view and still be respected by the rest of the group, since his or her loyalty to the organization has been established. People understand any quirks of personality or other differences and are now willing to accept the dissenter. They are open to listen. In the volunteer organization or local church, this kind of mutual respect is much more difficult to attain. If you have ever wondered why church committee meetings sometimes go so poorly, the reason lies here. Many business people become extremely frustrated about a volunteer committee's apparent inability to make decisions. They come from an organizational environment where decisions are made much more readily. What most of us do not realize is that it takes time to build relationships. Committees made up of volunteers need to spend a considerable amount of their precious time in the business of relating to one another.

Too often, such committees do not take the time to do this.

The wise leader will find ways of developing understanding and commonality among members of a group. This can be done by taking a group on a prayer retreat just to get to know one another. It can be done by setting aside times at the beginning of meetings for groups of two or three to get together to share one personal problem and pray for each other. (Avoid large-group prayer. Our experience is that most of us tend to pray *at* one another rather than *for* one another in these situations.) One of the keys to good group process is to put people together in small groups, so that during a given period of time a maximum amount of interaction and self-expression can go on. People are given enough time to be heard as well as to listen to other people.

Steps in Group Planning

It is important to see that the steps in the planning process need to be differentiated. If the phases overlap, individuals will be frustrated—and many times the planning exercise will fail. We recommend thinking about the *group* planning process as broken down into at least three major steps: (1) data gathering; (2) idea evaluation; and (3) integration of ideas into plans. In the *data gathering* phase, all of the group members have an opportunity to bring forth all of their ideas. In the *idea evaluation* phase, the ideas are sorted and compared. In the *integration* phase, the ideas are worked into plans.

DATA GATHERING

When we gather data as individuals, we continually integrate this new information into the existing situation without even thinking about the process. The human mind is amazingly adept at running ahead, or tracking back over past history, even while gaining new information. The best example of this is the tremendous amount of data processing that goes on while driving an automobile. We are continuously exposed to new information, primarily by what we see through the windshield. As this new information appears in front of us, we integrate it with our past experience and continually make new plans about what we are going to do in the future. We carry out this same kind of back-and-forth integration of data gathering and planning in many areas of life. It happens in both short-term and long-term events, and as we try to solve problems we find new avenues of success and may change our plans in midstream with very good effect.

But a group is seldom able to do this. If one person is still tracking over past history while another one is running ahead to the future, there will be a great deal of difficulty in communication. We need to agree as to where we are going to be at a given time. This is why it is so important (in the first steps of group planning) that data gathering be kept separate from problem solving and planning. When we speak of *group* planning, we are referring to a group which interacts together. What follows would not necessarily be true if a committee had given different assignments to different individuals who were going to bring all this information together for review. Then it might be very appropriate simultaneously to gather data and make recommendations about the consequences of this data. Our focus here is how to carry out a discussion among a group of people who are seeking to do some planning together. Thus, we recommend that the first step be data gathering, and that—regardless of what technique is used—the discussion be limited to just data, information, and facts, until the group has agreed to move on to the evaluation of the data.

The rules for group data gathering are quite similar to those of "brainstorming":

- Everyone has an opportunity to participate.
- Anything goes.
- Nothing is too large or too small for consideration.
- There is no evaluation or criticism of other people's ideas.
- Everyone builds on others' ideas.
- There is no necessary logic or sequence to the way that ideas are gathered.
- Participants should be able to know that their ideas have been heard.
- The results of the discussion should be displayed in a way that everyone can eventually see them.

We will discuss three group data-gathering approaches: the Slip Technique, the Newsprint Technique, and the Chalkboard Technique. Because we believe that the Slip Technique is the most effective of these and because it explains a great deal about how the others work, we will deal with this at length.

The Slip Technique. This is a way of helping a group of people gather information quickly, while utilizing the dynamics of group problem solving to bring to the surface ideas and/or information that might not otherwise appear. It uses the rules of traditional brainstorming. Instead of using secretaries to write ideas down as they are voiced, each individual writes down his suggestion as verbalized to the group. This permits a very rapid gathering of ideas and a free flow of information. The Slip Technique has the further advantage that each idea is written on a separate piece of paper, card, or slip. This later permits ideas to be arranged and rearranged in relationship to one another according to their importance and in the time sequence in which they may be used.

A variation of the Slip Technique is to use pregummed labels, making it possible to move quickly from the ideas to their semipermanent arrangement on a large piece of paper. Further refinement of this technique uses PERT labels (see next chapter), so that the results can be arranged into a PERT or logic diagram, a picture of how things fit together.

1. *Materials Needed.*   You will need slips of paper or cards, probably 3 x 5. If the ideas are to be arranged on corkboard, you may want to use larger slips of paper. Use pencils, not pens, if you are planning to use the results in any permanent way. (If the slips are just going to be used for preliminary listing, obviously you can use any writing instruments. Some people like to use felt markers, so that if ideas are posted on a wall, they can be read from a distance.) A table for everyone to sit around is desirable, since it helps the movement of ideas.

2. *Number of People.*   There is no theoretical limit to the number of people who can do this exercise together. However, experience shows that when it gets beyond eight, you will probably have too much confusion. We would suggest that, for instance, if you have a group of twelve, you divide it into two groups of six—or one group of six might do the Slip Technique while a larger group observes. After the first series of exercises has been completed, the observing group members can often contribute ideas of their own.

In any event, you need a group leader. You don't necessarily need someone who has been well trained in the technique, but rather someone who will be able to follow directions and in general be able to keep people playing according to the rules. It is assumed that the people who are using this technique have some common background or experience which will help them to relate to the exercise that they are going through.

3. *Procedure.*   Arrange people around a table, giving each participant a number of slips, probably no more than twenty. Make sure that each has a pencil. Appoint a group leader and state the problem to be worked on. This might be anything from the gathering of informa-

tion about a particular situation to listing the long-range goals of the organization. Make sure that people understand the rules of brainstorming.

There should be a minimum of discussion about what is being done. After the objective has been stated, the group leader should strictly limit his comments to such questions as: "What would have to happen before this?"—"Here is an idea. What other ideas fit in with this?"—"Fine! Write that down!" (The latter would be in response to whatever suggestion is made.) The group leader normally writes down the objective or the goal to be accomplished, reads it, and then again asks such questions as: "What has to happen before this?" or "What else has happened to make this happen?" As an individual responds, the group leader acknowledges each response by repeating it and adding, "Fine! Write that down!" There is no evaluation on his part—only affirmation.

Only the individual who suggested the idea writes it down. This is very important. While one individual is writing down an idea, other individuals can contribute their own suggestions. In this way, it is possible to have every member of the group writing down an idea at the same time. You have as many "secretaries" as participants.

Only *one* idea should be written on each slip of paper. As each individual writes down an item, he should then put this slip of paper aside and take a new slip of paper to be ready for the next idea that may come to mind. Ask people to use block lettering. Most people's handwriting is not easily read by others, especially when done rapidly.

Sometimes it is useful to place the slips in front of the group leader as they are written. In this way, if the group begins to falter, the group leader can pick up one slip, read it, and ask, "What would have to happen before this happens?" or "Here is an idea. Can you think of any others like it?" The group leader's questions will, of course, depend upon the category of information being handled. If you are trying to work out a plan, "What has to happen before this?" is appropriate. On the other hand, if you are gathering information about a particular person's job, the leader might ask, "What else does this person do?"

Continue with this procedure until it appears that the group has exhausted its ideas. Most of the time this will take no more than ten or fifteen minutes. Make sure that everyone is satisfied before you move on to the ordering and evaluating of ideas.

The Newsprint Technique. Because of the need to get ideas out where they can be seen, some people like to use newsprint or large sheets from an easel pad for data gathering. Sometimes two or three easels are used, each with a secretary. The idea is to display people's ideas where others can build on them. One advantage of putting ideas down in fairly large block letters on newsprint is that everybody can see the previous ideas and watch them build. This advantage can also be a distraction! Here, too, the group leader has to keep things moving to keep people from evaluating and questioning ideas. Again, remember the rules of brainstorming.

Another advantage of the newsprint technique is that two or three subgroups can be working on the same idea at the same time. Each can display its suggestions, and the groups can evaluate together what the others have done.

The Chalkboard Technique. Data may also be gathered on a chalkboard or overhead projector. This has the advantage of putting ideas down immediately where everybody can see them. The Chalkboard Technique has the disadvantage of moving slower, and it is difficult to rearrange the ideas once they have been recorded.

Other data-gathering techniques.   There are other useful data-gathering approaches that do not require the entire group to be present. One of these is the Delphi Technique. One person writes a report, scenario, or discussion about a situation, including how it might turn out and how it should be encountered with a plan. This report is then circulated to a number of other people who give their comments on whether or not they think the report is the right way to go and what they might suggest as alternatives. These alternatives are incorporated anonymously into a new report, which is in turn circulated to the same group. The process is continued until such time as all major differences are quite clear and the individual who holds a particular view has no more to contribute. The agreement or differences are clearly defined. This is a time-consuming approach, but it does result in some very thorough thinking.

Another form of data gathering is what we usually call "research," the search for a missing experience. This research can be anything from making some telephone calls to carrying out very formal experiments under controlled conditions, as might be done with a particular group within an organization. Do not overlook the uses of research by different individuals in the group. You could begin by taking the group through the Slip Technique to compile a list of all the things that you need to know. In other words, instead of coming up with solutions, come up with all of the questions that you need to ask. Then these questions can be assigned to individuals to report back at the next time together. In fact, if you will review the steps in problem solving described in chapter 9, you will see that this method of using the group to get as many concepts or ideas out as quickly as possible can be used at every step along the way. You are not only looking for answers; you are looking for questions. To put it another way, there are three kinds of data you want: correct questions, accurate background material to analyze, and the synthesis of this background experience into good solutions.

ORDERING AND EVALUATING IDEAS

So far we have discussed ways in which groups can *gather* ideas. Now we need some techniques that will help the group members to *evaluate* what they have done, with the hope of obtaining group consensus and ownership of a resulting plan.

Grouping the ideas.   The first step is to bring the ideas together in logical groups according to subject category. For example, suppose we are planning a training seminar. Logical groups of ideas might be those that relate to training materials, to the people who are going to be doing the presentations, to the facilities that are going to be used, and to the recruiting of seminar participants.

A second step in bringing ideas together is *in terms of importance*. In the data-gathering phase, some very insignificant suggestions may have been made during the excitement and fun of writing down different ideas. Usually these will become obvious, and the people who are responsible for them will not feel badly about having them put aside. If all of the ideas are first brought together by category and then evaluated for importance by the group, the insignificant ideas will easily appear. Obviously, a system of prioritizing is needed. In the next chapter, we discuss the ABC Technique of evaluating. We think that you will find this a useful and easy system. It takes the pressure off having to rank ideas in a 1-2-3 manner and makes it possible to rank ideas by groups.

After ideas have been grouped by type and ranked by

priority or importance, the next step is to *order them in time*. Some ideas in the plan will be time-dependent upon others. In other words, event *C* may not be possible until we have completed events *A* and *B*. (In our later discussion on PERT, you can see how this logic works.)

In putting pairs of ideas together in relationship to each another, you may uncover goals or events that conflict. In other words, it may not be possible for the organization to buy into both ideas and be consistent with its own overall purposes. Situations like this are not always easy to resolve. You may have to analyze why these suggestions do or do not fit in with your basic purpose. At other times the ABC Technique will quickly put one to the side. Again, the important thing is to try to involve the group in the discussion, using methods such as those described under the Slip Technique to try to keep things under control. This is a lot easier to say than it is to do. However, if you have established some procedure or game rules for how you will proceed, you make it a lot easier for those involved.

Idea arrangement and the Slip Technique.   If you were trying to gather information about a job for the purposes of writing a job description, you might ask everybody in a department or committee what a particular person in that section does. The first question might be: "What does Arlene do for you or the organization?" In this situation, you might want to arrange the material by categories, and it would be quite simple to do so. Using the Slip Technique, this can also be done in a group by asking one person what category of material his top slip represents. For instance, a person might discover that Arlene "helps with the payroll." The group leader would then ask all the other individuals in the group if they had written anything that had to do with Arlene's work on payroll. If they had, they would pass their slips to the person who had the first suggestion. In this way, various categories of information can be stacked together rather quickly.

When the Slip Technique is used for planning, we need to see how all the different events that have been suggested fit together into some cohesive plan, how they relate to one another. There is a basic assumption that the group has all of the information needed to find the best way to reach a goal. The task now is to see which ideas support which other ideas and in what sequence these events have to take place in order to reach our goal. It will often not be possible to have the entire group participate in the ordering of ideas, since this may get too confusing. Usually, a maximum of three people should carry out this work.

Idea slips can be moved in time sequence from left to right, or in patterns or chains of events, using a large sheet of paper as a background. They can then be arranged in like categories. While this is being done, the individuals who are doing the arranging can see the plan or idea developing. Often this will raise a question: "What about such-and-such? We completely left that off." At this point, another slip can be written and added to those that are already there. When the slips are in appropriate order, they can be glued or taped to the paper. Another way of arranging the ideas is to tack them on a corkboard, letting everyone see them from a distance. This has the disadvantage of taking larger slips of paper and more space.

Idea evaluation.   As the group goes through the procedure, it will usually become obvious that some ideas are much too general or much too small to be put in a category with others. In teaching this material, as an exercise we used to ask people to "think about all of the things needed to build a bridge." (We had to learn the hard way that it is difficult for people to plan something that they know very little about!) In the midst of this, someone would say something such as, "Let's have a Miss Bridge contest!" The obvious response was, "Fine, write that down!"

"Let's have a ribbon-cutting ceremony."

"Fine, write that down!"

"Then we'll need a ribbon."

"Fine, write that down!"

"Then we'll need scissors."

"Fine, write that down!" (although at this point the group leader's enthusiasm was beginning to wane).

When it came time to sort out ideas, it would be apparent to all that the acquiring of a pair of scissors to cut a ribbon was probably not in the same category as preparing the main foundation of the bridge. In other words, there must be a balance to the magnitude of ideas to be considered. In the case of getting the job description for Arlene, probably the fact that she cleaned her typewriter would be too small a detail—while the fact that Arlene came to work each day would be too general. The group will usually see this, and even the person who suggested a particular idea will feel quite comfortable with putting it aside.

Idea integration.   The ordering of ideas can be done in relation to their *importance* (culling out the unimportant ones as we just mentioned). It can be done in terms of *kind:* all of the things that have to do with the preparation for a meeting, the conducting of a meeting, and/or the cleaning up afterwards. It can be done in terms of *time:* those things which have to be done immediately and those not necessary until sometime in the future. How the ideas are ordered will depend upon how they are going to be displayed. We will discuss this next.

DISPLAYING OF IDEAS

A major factor in the use of the Slip Technique is that it facilitates permitting all of those who participated in the work to see their ideas appear. This gives a sense of group ownership in what has been done, another key concept. It is also important that the ideas be displayed in a way that is not too cumbersome and is as compact as possible. For example, one of the difficulties with placing all of the ideas on a time line or calendar sequence is that if you are planning two years' work, the length of paper needed can get rather considerable. We will give a number of examples of how to arrange and display ideas. In some cases they will be worthy of a separate discussion in another chapter.

Random list.   The first and most obvious approach is to put the ideas together in some kind of random list. This might be done by just listing them one after another. A good improvement on this is to order them by groups or kinds. Here you might find it possible to list all the statements on one or two pieces of standard-sized typing paper. You might want to edit them slightly. Sometimes an individual will write down a single word which may need interpretation. For example, in planning a training curriculum, someone might write down the word *workbook*. You might have to add a verb to that to make the listing "acquire workbook binders."

Project list.   A further step is to try to relate ideas to time and people. In the next chapter (see Figure 17), we have suggested a simple form that you could use. You will note that this has the advantage of describing *what* the event or the idea is, *who* is responsible for it, and *when* the event has to be completed. This approach assumes that we are doing planning and that there is some time sequence involved for the ideas that have been gathered.

The Gantt Chart. A further refinement for displaying ideas gathered in planning is the Gantt Chart. This is also illustrated and discussed in the next chapter (see Figure 18).

PERT: the logic diagram. This is the next obvious approach. (Actually, a Gantt Chart is also a form of logic diagram.) In the next chapter we discuss in detail the use of a particular type of logic diagram known as PERT (Program Evaluation and Review Technique), which many people have found useful.

Choice of display method. If you are gathering ideas in terms of historical events, you might want to assemble them in the form of a narrative history. A simple list might be used if you are gathering ideas on people's assumptions about the world or about the organization. If you are gathering ideas for prayer, you might want to arrange them in logical categories. Try to fit the display to the needs of the group. If you plan to share all the information at a congregational meeting, you will want to get it down in a compact and easily read manner. If you are using it for committee work, you might be satisfied with an agenda list of items which need further work. The most important thing to remember is that ideas need to be displayed. They must be fed back to the people who initiated them. This moves the entire group along in ownership of the goals and suggestions.

Adaptability of the Slip Technique

The Slip Technique is particularly adaptable to work in volunteer groups. It is very useful in helping committees to hear each other's ideas and to get these ideas out rapidly. Following the sequence of our overall approach discussed in chapter 12, this method could be used for:

1. Gathering ideas about the purpose of the organization

2. Gathering ideas about the goals that support the purposes
3. Prioritizing the goals to discover which are the most important
4. Gathering ideas and events to support the selected goals and to discover and write plans
5. Listing all the difficulties we seem to be facing in overcoming a problem
6. Listing ideas that might contribute to the solution of a problem
7. Evaluating past performance in terms of good and bad results

Practical uses.   A very neat, rather simple use of the Slip Technique is to get a *listing of materials* that might be needed in order to carry out a program or to proceed with the solving of a problem. Sometimes you will want to use the Slip Technique to *recall history.* The question here would be: "What has happened in the past that we need to recall now?"

An often overlooked planning need is to *list assumptions.* Here the question would be: "What assumptions do we have—about ourselves, the world, our organization—that need to be stated at this time?" Don't overlook the use of the technique for *gathering items for prayer.* This will quickly uncover individual needs.

The technique can be used to discover *who is responsible for what.* Here the question will be: "What are all of the things that Bill is responsible for?" (Bill might not agree that he is responsible for all of these things!)

The Slip Technique can also help *uncover a problem:* "What questions need to be answered before we are able to move on to solving the problem?" In other words, "What is the problem?" At other times you need to *gather ideas on the problems that need to be overcome.* In this case, the question is: "What problems do you see that we are going to have to overcome in order to reach this goal?"

Finally, one of the most useful ways of using the Slip Technique is in *making plans*. In this case, it is assumed that the goal is understood. Ideas for plans are gathered as "events."

Advantages. There are many advantages to this technique. Probably the most important is that the Slip Technique takes advantage of the knowledge of the group, while at the same time gives the group a feeling of participation in what is going on. This logically leads to people's owning of any solutions that emerge from the procedure.

It helps people to see where they fit. Many times they will not have understood that they have a role to play, and the listing of ideas that involve them helps them to feel the affirmation of others. Similarly, the technique tends to draw out people who would normally be silent and helps to silence those people who might be over-talkative, by giving everyone the opportunity to express ideas in rather simple and nondebatable ways. As a consequence, it helps people to value one another and respect the ideas of others.

Cautions. There are a few cautions that probably need to be noted. First, make sure that the group has some reasonable cohesiveness in terms of what is going to be discussed. We too often make the assumption that everyone knows what is going on. For instance, in using this with a new committee in a church, you might want to pick a subject that you are sure is going to be familiar to everyone. We suggest practicing on some rather unimportant things. In our seminars, we have searched for a "sample project" that might be common to almost all of the participants. Following the lead of the Laubach Literacy organization, we have used the preparation of an English muffin as a practice for data gathering and planning. The stated goal is "Toasted, buttered, jellied English muffin served."

Further Reading

God's Purpose and Man's Plans by Edward R. Dayton. (See reading list for chapter 5.)
Joining Together: Group Theory and Group Skills by David W. Johnson and Frank P. Johnson. (See reading list for chapter 12.)

15

Planning Tools

Be diligent to present yourself approved to God as a workman who does not need to be ashamed, handling accurately the word of truth.

2 Timothy 2:15

Group planning has great advantages, particularly in the nonprofit or volunteer organizations, such as the local church. However, when it comes to refining plans—taking into account all of the factors and shaping them into forms that will easily communicate what is intended—this is best done by individuals who are specifically skilled and assigned to the task. In this chapter we will detail three ways of displaying plans—simple lists, the bar graph or Gantt Chart, and PERT (Program Evaluation and Review Technique). We will discuss the impact of prioritizing and the simple technique for doing this, as well as scheduling and assigning time in order to carry out the plan. Finally, we will conclude with a discussion on evaluation.

Displaying Plans

There are many different ways of displaying your plans. The important thing is to make sure that they *are* displayed. A major purpose of planning is to show people where they fit into what the organization is doing, and how the results of somebody else's work is going to have an impact on them.

Some years ago, we built a new building on our World Vision property. The builder posted a Gantt Chart (see Figure 18) on the wall near the entrance to the old building. Here he kept track of progress as things moved along. Everyone involved could see what the builder thought was happening in terms of his plans. Although he ran into material difficulties which caused him to replan, the fact that he had the courage to display his plans gave everyone a feeling of understanding where he was in the process.

In a similar way, it is useful to display plans for the entire group. At times, after the ideas have been gathered and evaluated and posted onto a plan, individuals will be surprised that they turned out that way. This is all the more reason for putting things together in a way which will display the interrelationships. People can then indicate any disagreement or misunderstanding.

Plans can be anything from a simple list to very elaborate PERT logic diagrams. In many ways, even a calendar can be a plan. You might want to list on a standard calendar all of the events that had to do with a particular program. For instance, suppose you were planning a year's training program and there was quite a bit of detail that had to be carried on during the first three months. You could list all of these items on a monthly calendar. But there are more effective ways of displaying your plans . . . .

Simple list of needs. In order to show the effect of different displays, we will use as an example the planning of a seminar. In 1970, when we first began to do management training as a team, we found it necessary to consider all the things that would be needed in order to put on a management seminar in a distant city. We went through the brainstorming technique already discussed and then listed all the events that we could think of. Our list looked something like this:

Prepare tentative budget
Choose location
List potential speakers available
Prepare special texts
Write program outline
Notify prospective attendees adequately
Make available special binders and texts
Obtain publicity
Approve budget
Establish advertising and promotion plan
Decide on dates
Complete direct-mail brochure
Contact and commit speakers
Work out public-relations program
Establish seminar fees
List aids required by speakers
Make available a final list of attendees

Chronological project list. Another way would be to make a list of the events, showing the individuals responsible for each and the dates to begin and complete them. We have shown such a list—for planning the same seminar—in Figure 17. The items are listed in the order of completion. The advantage of such a list, particularly if it can be kept to an 8½-by-11 piece of paper, is that items can be crossed off as you move along. Interim photocopies of the list can be sent to all the people involved, thus providing progress reports. Another advantage of this chart is that everyone can see who is responsible for what. These are the *goal owners*. As previously mentioned, in order for a plan to be operational, someone must own each task and see himself as responsible for it. This form assigns such responsibilities. A disadvantage of this project list is that it does not show the

ITEM NO	DESCRIPTION	RESPONSIBLE PERSON Brown	James	Rogers	Kuajle	Johnson			SCHEDULE Begin	Complete
	List of potential speakers	X							—	1/2/73
	Tentative budget prepared				X				1/2/73	1/10/73
	Program outline written		X						1/15/73	1/21/73
	Location chosen				X				1/19/73	1/22/73
	Contacting of speakers begun	X							1/8/73	1/22/73
	Contract given				X				1/22/73	2/8/73
	Break-even set					X			2/5/73	2/12/73
	Speakers committed	X							1/2/73	3/15/73
	Start texts		X						2/15/73	—
	Special binders ordered		X						1/21/73	2/20/73
	Program designed	X							3/15/73	2/27/73
	Advertising plan established	X							2/15/73	2/27/73
	Floor plan drawn				X				2/26/73	3/3/73
	List assembled	X							2/15/73	3/4/73
	Order print on texts		X						3/8/73	—
	Direct mail brochures completed		X						2/27/73	3/15/73
	Special binders received	X							2/20/73	3/23/73
	1st mailing	X							3/4/73	3/25/73
	1st registration			X					3/25/73	4/1/73
	List equipment				X				4/1/73	4/8/73
	Final cost fixed					X			3/25/73	4/8/73
	Texts available		X						—	4/13/73

Figure 17

impact of one person's failure to execute his part of the plan.

The Gantt Chart.   Another method of displaying plans is represented by the Gantt Chart (Figure 18) which involves grouping tasks together within several categories. This is essentially a bar graph and its use in planning that same seminar is illustrated in Figure 18.

PLANNING FOR Managing Your Time Seminar — Preparation

TASK	SCHEDULE (Months, weeks, days)						TOTAL COST (FIXED)	
	JAN	FEB	MAR	APR	MAY	JUNE	MIN	MAX
SPEAKERS	Possible speakers / Speakers contacted	Speakers committed					750	1,000
PROGRAM DESIGN	Outline	Start texts	Organize point / Notes / Binders	Tests available / (Binders rcvd)			800	950
PUBLICITY			Program designed	Press releases received / 1st release	Last release		150	200
PROMOTIONAL MATERIAL		Advertising plan / Brochure	List assembled 1st mail	2nd mailing / 3rd mail			650	800
REGISTRATION				1st registrations / 1st reg rat'l mailed	Close registrations	Roster of attendees	300	400
FACILITY	Select site	Contract	Floor plan		Select meals / Seating	Final check	200	250
EQUIPMENT				List equipment / Locate	Order / Test	Deliver	100	200
BUDGET	Tentative	Break-even set		Final fixed cost		Last collection		

TOTAL   2950   3800

Probable Cost FIXED   3400

Description: All Preparation needed to put on a two-day M.Y.T. Seminar on June 15–16 in Los Angeles

Prepared for ___MARC___ by ___(signature)___ Date Nov 6, 72

Figure 18

Here, different kinds of needs have been grouped together: speakers, program design, publicity, promotion, registration, facility, equipment, budget. An unshaded bar drawn on the chart shows when the first event for each of these categories will be begun and the last completed. Each of the events is represented along the bar by a triangle which is filled in as completed. As time passes, the bar continuum is also filled in.

Figure 18 shows the situation as of about February 20. Note that the triangles for all events scheduled up to that date have been filled in, except for "binders" (Program Design) and "contract" (Budget). This type of chart shows us immediately which events are behind schedule and which are complete, as well as which are to happen next.

The advantage of this display is that it shows a great deal of information in a very small package. Progress can be shown as time passes, and everyone can have an overall picture of what is happening. The disadvantage of the Gantt Chart is that it does not relate events to people. However, in some cases, if one person is responsible for an entire phase (such as Speakers), his name could be included in the block under "task."

PERT logic diagram. Finally, there is the logic diagram or PERT chart (Figure 19). In our experience, if people like this, it works very well. Use it only if it seems to fit. Modify if it seems advisable. The PERT diagram was originally designed to show the relationship of very complex programs, but it is useful in displaying almost any kind of plan. You can see how it is a natural step from the Slip Technique. Each event is located with relationship to other events in time. In other words, any event to the left of one event must have happened before that one. Any event to the right happens after the particular event under consideration. The rela-

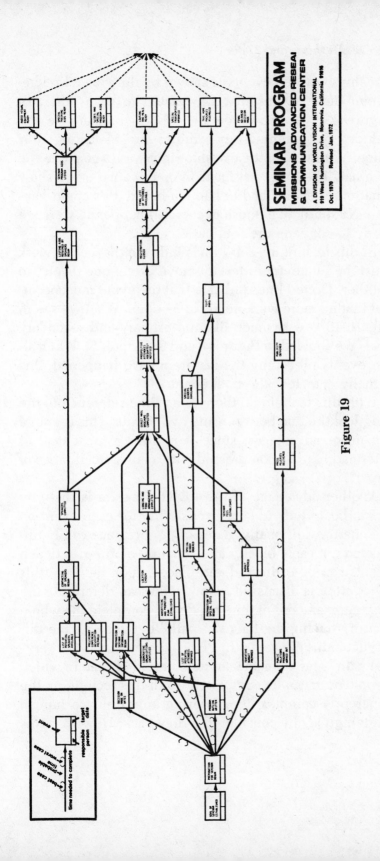

Figure 19

tionship between events is shown by drawing a line between those events that are related to each other. In Figure 19, we show you the PERT diagram we developed for planning our seminar on "Managing Your Time." Our goal at the extreme right was to convene the seminar. The lines that focus in on this final event show what other events had to happen before this could happen. Not until all of those events had happened were we ready to convene the seminar.

In this technique, solid lines indicate that actual work must be done in order to move from one event to another. Dotted lines indicate that the event must occur, but that no more work needs to be done. What we see in Figure 19 is very much like the primary and secondary goals we showed in Figures 8 and 9 (chapter 5). When all the events preceding the last item have happened, this actually "creates" the final event.

With this technique, there is no time reference to the length of the line between any two events. This is one of the major advantages, since it permits a great deal of information to be compressed onto a fairly small piece of paper.

Another advantage of the PERT diagram is that you can indicate individual responsibility for each event on the chart. Additionally, dates of performance can be indicated in each block. The amount of time between events can be estimated and placed upon the line (this scheduling is discussed below). One can determine the maximum amount of time needed to complete the whole plan by tracing the longest "path" between all the different chains of events. In PERT jargon, this is the "critical path" and gives the shortest period of time in which the program can be completed. With this technique, the apparently complex "engineering approach" to human planning may be considered a drawback. However, this

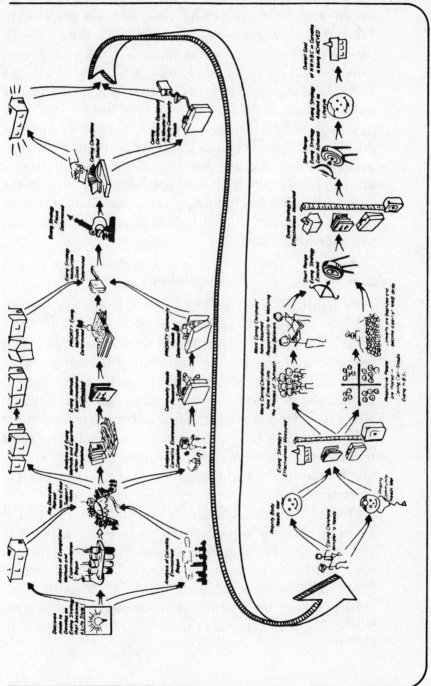

Figure 20

does not necessarily have to be the case. In Figure 20, we have reproduced a PERT chart that was made into a kind of flow diagram by one church, to show how its outreach program was going to work. Here you can see how an artist has made what might have appeared to be a rather cold and rigid plan come alive by showing people and events in symbolic and figurative form.

Use of the PERT diagram is covered in *God's Purpose and Man's Plans* (Dayton). If you are planning to use this approach, we suggest that you get a copy of this or another book on PERT before you begin. Again, as in the case of the Slip Technique, practice on some unimportant or imaginary project before applying this to your organization's plans.

Scheduling

Probably the most difficult part of planning is estimating how long it will take to accomplish something. Most of us have been involved at one time or another with a committee in which there were four or five assignments made and everyone started working on his assignment as soon as the initial committee meeting was over. Later on we may have discovered that one person's assignment was a two-day job, while another's responsibility was a two-month project. We had not stopped to consider how much time and human energy was going to be needed to carry something out.

One of the advantages of PERT planning is that it gives us a graphic way of displaying how much time it is going to take between events. You will notice that on each of the lines between events there is a pair of brackets. How these are used will be discussed below.

In planning terms, time is made up of two components. The first component is the quantity of energy—in terms of person-hours—that is going to be required to carry out a task. The second component is the scheduling. Based upon the number of person-hours required and the number of people available, what will be the elapsed or scheduled time required? Most of us tend to think about scheduled time rather than real hours.

How can we find out what is the likely amount of time that we are going to take? One way is to consider four different types of estimates: (1) expected time; (2) worst-case time; (3) best-case time; and (4) probable time. To illustrate, let us take an example of someone who is to prepare a slide presentation for a particular program. The first question to him might be: "Jim, how long do you think it will take to get this slide presentation completed?" Jim might respond, "Well, I think it can be done in about three weeks." This is the *expected* time.

The next two questions can give us the worst and best possible times: "Jim, if everything went just *right,* how long would it take?" Jim might respond, "Well, if everything went really right, I could do it in a little more than two weeks." This is the *best-case* time.

"Jim, if everything went *wrong,* how long would it take?" is our next question. This time Jim might respond, "Oh, my! If everything went wrong, it might take seven or eight weeks!" This is the *worst-case* time.

It is obvious that the *probable* time is not the same as the *expected* time. What the probable time really is will be based upon your estimation of what Jim is saying in his description of what could go wrong and what could go right. The important thing is that by asking someone for the *expected* time, the *best* possible time (usually asked first), and the *worst* possible time, we are more likely to arrive at the most *probable* time. The spaces on our PERT diagram in Figure 19 are there for us to put in the worst possible time, the probable time, and the best time.

If Jim is going to take on the entire responsibility—either because he has his own organization or because he will recruit others—perhaps it is not important for us to know how much energy (person-hours) he is going to expend. However, if Jim is working for our organization (which may have to pay the salaries of the people involved), one way of finding out how much time Jim is planning to spend is to ask him what the labor cost is going to be. This is also relevant to those working in volunteer organizations. Probably the questions to be asked of Jim in that case are: "Who is going to help you, Jim?" and "How long will you need them?" We may discover that Jim is planning to use some people who are already overworked, or people who we were planning to use in some other place.

Finally, we need to integrate and draw some kind of a relationship between the many aspects of the plan on which we are working. We need to make sure our plan is not going to interfere with someone else's plan. Otherwise, how easy it would be for the music committee or the choir director to plan to put on a church cantata using twenty-five people whom someone else is planning to use for an evangelistic outreach!

To sum up, scheduling is composed of both elapsed time and the amount of energy to be used. We need to set dates for each event being planned as a step to our goal. It is only when we have these events nailed down in terms of dates that we are able to carry out an effective evaluation.

Setting Priorities

In chapter 6 we discussed a general philosophy of priorities for a Christian organization. We set forth our general view that the Bible calls us first to a commitment to God and Christ, second to a commitment to one another in the Body of Christ, and third to the work of Christ. Specifically, how do you go about sorting out goals—deciding which are the most important and which are of less significance?

Priority considerations. All priority questions are first about "When?" In other words, we are faced with whether we are going to do this first, second, third, or perhaps never. By assigning such time ratings to events, we essentially put them in terms of priorities. In other words, priorities describe what we are going to do first.

This leads to the natural statement that we need to choose the future over the past. By this we mean that we should let our priorities be determined by the future that lies ahead rather than by the history that lies behind. Over the Archives Building in Washington is the phrase WHAT IS PAST IS PROLOGUE. This says it well.

Here is a list of questions that you might want to ask in trying to establish where something fits in order of priority for your organization:

1. *How urgent is it? When must it be done? Does it have to be done right now, today, soon, or someday?*— When you ask this question, you may discover that something doesn't have to be done at all!

2. *How important is it? Very important? Quite important? Somewhat important? Not so important?*—It is useful to note here that there is always a tension between the important and the urgent. Dwight D. Eisenhower was quoted as saying that important things are seldom urgent, and urgent things are seldom important. But it is the urgent things that keep getting in the way of the important things, is it not? We are always faced with those things that have to be done "right now." The urgent often turns out to be the enemy of the important.

3. *How often must it be done? Is it something that's done every day? Only occasionally? Or just sometimes?*—This will give us some insight as to how dependent we are on this event's occurrence.

4. *Can someone else or some other organization do it just as well?*—The answer might be *no, perhaps,* or *yes.* If the answer is *yes,* perhaps we should not be involved at all, but should turn the idea and suggestion over to some other committee, department, or organization.

5. *Is it part of a larger task to which we are committed?*—Very often we can get involved in goals which are attractive for the moment, but which really have nothing to do with our organization. This is probably the most subtle trap of all. How easy it is to get involved in "interesting" projects, which really do not relate to where we hope our organization is moving!

6. *What will happen if it's not done at all? What will happen if we abandon this whole goal? Disaster? Trouble? Difficulty? Nothing?*—If nothing will happen, perhaps we have a clue that we shouldn't be involved in it in the first place.

7. *Is this the best way?*—There will always be alternatives. But after we have decided upon one, we need to ask this final question.

The ABC Technique.   Assuming that you have a long list of goals and have made some evaluation of each one, how do you go about comparing goal with goal? Sometimes it feels almost as if we're trying to compare apples with oranges. If you have had the experience of trying to answer a questionnaire on which you were given ten ideas to rate in order of importance, you know how difficult this is. Multiply that by ten and you can see how almost impossible it is to take a list of a hundred goals and try to rank them. It is not only very difficult to hold so many ideas in the mind at one time, but you are also faced with the fact that if a certain goal is number one, it follows that every other goal can be no better than number two. In real life, things do not turn out that way, since there are often a number of goals that are "number one."

Here is a procedure to break down a large list of goals into a usable chunk. It is called the ABC Technique. It also might be called "Divide and Conquer," or the "Salami Technique," a way of taking a whole and dividing it up into smaller pieces.

We suggest that you divide your list into three categories—*A, B,* and *C*—by the following criteria:

A—"Must do." This is something that is very important, something to which you would give high value.

B—"Should do." These are things that have some importance, to which you would give medium value.

C—"Can do." These are things that you don't necessarily have to do. These things are not so important, and you would give them a low value.

With the list before you or a group of people, go through the items and categorize all the things that are *A*'s. You do not have to spend very much time on this. Just ask yourself, "Is this an *A*?" If it isn't, pass it by and go on to the next one. A group can do this together very well, as long as the members have a common understanding of what they are discussing. In this case, *A*'s would only be things about which every member of the group felt positive. If there was any negative response, you would pass it by for the next time around. In this way you can go down a list of a hundred goals and probably find fifteen or twenty which you would categorize as *A*'s.

Now repeat the procedure with *C*'s. Start at the top again (passing all the *A*'s) and go down the list. Again, if you're working with a group, don't accept a *C* rating unless everyone in the group agrees that it is a *C*. When you have finished this, everything that remains must be a *B*! But it's a good idea to check. Go down the list with the group members again and make sure they all agree that these are no better than a *B*.

Now it may turn out that you have too many *A* goals. Perhaps half of your total turned out to be "must do," and you want to try to refine the list further. In order to do this, take all of the *A*'s and review by asking yourself the same set of questions for this new grouping: "Is this an *A*, *B*, or *C*?" You will discover that you can go through this quite rapidly. When you're through, you will probably have two or three items which you might call *AA*, with others being categorized as *AB* or *AC*. Obviously, this is a simple technique for helping the group to see what it values and to uncover those goals that it wants to work on *first*.

Using Facilitators or Enablers

Many times an outsider can play a key role in helping an organization regain its momentum or start it on its way. This is particularly true if the outsider is viewed as an "enabler" or "facilitator," rather than as an "expert" in the group's particular situation. He or she will be viewed as someone who comes with no axe to grind or preconceived ideas as to what ultimate directions the organization should take.

This person's skills should lie in the area of group process and group dynamics. The outsider should be sensitive to the felt needs of the organization and must be very careful about injecting personal biases. Fortunately, the demand for such facilitators or enablers has been growing, and there is a reasonably large cadre of such individuals available, both from denominational groups and from organizations which have been established specifically to carry out such a role.

Whether you need such a person will depend upon the

expertise found within the organization and the amount of time which you have to get your process moving. In discussing your situation with potential facilitators, you need to be frank and open about both your needs and your ability to pay for the services rendered.

Evaluation

The idea of planning is to point the way, so we can see when we have departed from it. No plan will ever be exactly as it should be, and plans should be displayed with the idea that we will evaluate progress against them and change them if they are not of value to us.

This means that evaluation needs to be built into plans, and we must assign this responsibility to someone. One of the main reasons for having meetings (see next chapter) is to assess progress. If no evaluation is made, we are going to get much less out of our planning than we should. Just as planning and problem solving go hand in hand, so do planning and evaluation. Plans are a statement of what we intend to do. Evaluation tells us how we are doing against those plans. Problem solving may be needed to rewrite a plan or to find out another way of approaching a new obstacle.

Expect plans to change. Planning should be thought of as an arrow which points direction. There is nothing wrong with changing our plans. In fact, a good display system should have built into it a way of showing such changes.

Further Reading

The Art of Management for Christian Leaders by Ted W. Engstrom and Edward R. Dayton. (See reading list for chapter 1.)

Tools for Time Management by Edward R. Dayton.

God's Purpose and Man's Plans by Edward R. Dayton (see reading list for chapter 5) has a full description of how to use PERT.

16

Meetings

He who neglects discipline despises himself, But he who listens to reproof acquires understanding.
                                        Proverbs 15:32

Meetings are what life is all about! Discussions between individuals and groups help us to understand what has been done, what is being done now, and where we may be moving in the future. Despite the importance of meetings, nobody seems to have much good to say about them. Everybody goes to them, and many of us spend a good deal of our lives there. Unfortunately, not many of us understand the human dynamics of meetings.

We need to think of meetings as being the lifeblood of an organization. We can carry on a great deal of an organization's day-to-day operations through written correspondence, and yet the most important aspects of organizational life are the give-and-take between people who are able to "read" each other, even while the communication is taking place. The English language is such that it depends a great deal on the inflection of the voice and the emphasis that is placed on different words and sentences for us to grasp what is intended in the communication. Too often we misread memos and letters because we bring to the reading of them an entirely different viewpoint or bias from what the author intended. So we need meetings. We need to rejoice over them and should make them as useful and effective as possible.

Meetings can be classified in a number of ways, all of which are useful to us as we try to make them more effective. We are going to limit ourselves here to the task-oriented meeting, as opposed to the fellowship meeting. We will discuss what happens when two or more people come together to accomplish something outside of themselves. Their primary purpose is not fellowship.

Why Meetings Go Wrong

Most of us have had the experience of sitting in a church meeting with a group of men and women who are extremely competent in the various enterprises of which they are a part. These are people who know how to "get things done" in their own business or profession. And yet, for some reason, in the meetings held by the church or other volunteer organization, they just don't seem to be able to make those same things happen. Volunteers and lay people in the church can become tremendously frustrated by this kind of leadership. Why is this so? Why is it that meetings of volunteer groups never seem to measure up to the efficiency of meetings in the business organization?

The primary reason is that the participants fail to realize that in their business meetings they are usually very familiar with the people with whom they are meeting. They work with them daily. They pass them in the hall, have lunch together, generally understand each other's weaknesses and strengths, and know each other's reputations. Consequently, when they come to a meeting together, they see each other as *whole* people. Contrast this with a typical church board which may have twelve individuals who meet together once a month for an hour or two. Although some of them may have social relationships within and outside the church, most of them may not know each other in terms of their working roles. Consequently, communication will be hindered and the ability of the participants to make progress will be greatly reduced.

What can we do to overcome this? Obviously, we need first to build in relationships and learn to know one another at a deeper level. There are a number of ways of doing this. One way is to break up the participants into groups of three before each meeting and have them share one request they will pray about until the next time the group meets. After they have shared, they can pray for one another. At the time of the next meeting, the same group of three comes together again and shares the results of what happened to them during this time, as they have prayed. They then form into another group of three and repeat the process. In this way, individuals will come much closer over a period of a year. Another way of getting past this difficulty is to take the entire committee on some form of retreat, where members can see one another in a setting other than that of the meeting room. In any event, remember the priorities that we laid out in chapter 6. If the body of believers is to become effective, it must first become the *Body* of Christ.

Kinds of Meetings

Meetings can be classified as formal or informal, which is probably another way of saying that some meetings are planned ahead of time and many more are impromptu and "just happen."

Another way of classifying meetings is by the terms *special* or *ongoing*. By the latter we mean that some meetings are set up on a continuing basis. Such a regular meeting of a committee or group is, to a large degree, *ongoing* and a continuation of the one that preceded it. Each meeting is based upon the one that has gone before and is seen as part of a process. A *special* meeting, on the other hand, is one called to handle a specific problem or situation. It may be made up of a cohesive group, but it is not anticipated at the time of the meeting that it is part of an overall pattern.

A third way of classifying meetings is described in the book *Creative Management* by Norman Maier and John Hayes. They point out that meetings can be described in terms of their general purpose and identify three basic kinds of meetings: (1) one that is called to announce or inform people; (2) one called to obtain the support of the group (a decision having been already made); and (3) one called for problem solving, at which it is expected that everyone will get involved in the discussion with the idea of arriving at a consensus or a solution.

This interesting book gives some excellent examples of what happens when an individual thinks that he is at a problem-solving meeting, when in reality he is at one of the other kinds. You have probably had this kind of experience yourself. The leadership of a committee calls a meeting "to discuss the location of a new building." You go to the meeting, assuming that the decision as to where the building is to be placed is still in question and that the leaders are looking for information. In reality, the location has already been decided upon. It has been checked out with most concerned. The purpose of the meeting is really to obtain general consensus that this is indeed the right way to go. In other words, the question is not "Where shall we place the building?" but rather "Is *this* the best place?" If you enter the meeting and want to discuss other places to locate the building, you are quickly going to create disorder within the meeting—and probably a great deal of unhappiness within yourself. Of course this type of affirmation (or "blessing") meeting has a real place in the life of an organization. The important thing is to make sure that everyone understands the kind of a meeting being attended.

Meetings Have a Poor Image

Meetings form a very real part of our society, and yet they have a rather poor track record in the minds of most people. We are all familiar with the definition of a camel as "a horse that was designed by a committee." The existence of so many camels, wandering about the wastelands of many Christian organizations, is testimony to the fact that we need to learn a great deal more about the dynamics involved. Meetings are interpersonal intersection points and are particularly *human* events. They are consuming of human energies and time and consequently need to be viewed with a great deal more loving care than most of us give to them.

The Elements of Any Good Meeting

It is quite simple to spell out the elements of a good meeting, but much harder to carry them out.

1. *Know the purpose of the meeting.* Where does it fit in the overall structure of the organization or the situation in which we are? If we don't understand the real "Why?" of the meeting and where it fits, we are not very likely to use the meeting well.

2. *Set goals.* What is it that is to be accomplished during this encounter? How will we know that this happened?

3. *Select the right participants.* Who needs to contribute what? Who does not need to be invited to this particular meeting? Are there some outsiders or outside skills that are going to be required?

4. *Do your homework* (and encourage other participants to do theirs). We are all familiar with conferences of Christian executives at which it appears that most of the people have done their work on the airplane en route. A good meeting is one in which the ongoing nature of the meeting forms a good foundation for what is to

follow, or for which someone has done a good job of laying out a position for all to understand *before* they come. We don't need meetings at which to read and listen to papers. Most of us are able to read much more effectively by ourselves. But if we have done our homework, we can really get down to the business of discussing what was found in the papers.

5. *Select the right location.* The environment in which a meeting is carried out says a great deal about the meeting. The care with which you prepare is an important tool. Attention must be paid to the room layout, the availability of supplies, the many things that tell people that it is a good meeting.

6. *Bring adequate communication tools and resources.* If you are going to need an overhead projector and easel, make sure they are there.

7. *Prepare an agenda.* Adequately inform everyone as to what is going to happen. Use the agenda as a motivational tool in keeping the meeting moving toward the goal.

8. *Keep the meeting moving in the right direction.* By this is meant where it is *supposed* to be headed. If a diversion is necessary, announce to the participants that the goal of the meeting has been changed. It makes everyone very nervous when you have an agenda of ten items and, with only ten minutes left, you are only on item two.

9. *Announce what has been accomplished* (at the meeting's conclusion) and who is responsible for taking the next steps. Also announce what questions are still unresolved.

10. *Announce what action is to be taken in the future* (to handle what items are unresolved). Record and distribute "action items" at the end of the meeting.

How specific and detailed you will be in using these major elements will, of course, depend upon the meeting. However, even for an impromptu or informal meeting, it is a good idea to at least write down the goal and apparent facts and agree on these before you begin. Review the steps on problem solving (chapter 9). It is also a good idea at this time to decide what time you will adjourn.

Creative agendas. There are a number of ways of having useful agendas. For the ongoing meeting, a continuous list of action items can often serve as a good agenda. At the first meeting of a committee, items needing future attention or problems needing solution can be listed on a piece of paper with the date on which each item was first set down. As each item is resolved, it is crossed off and the date of its resolution noted. The same paper is then reproduced and distributed as the agenda for the next meeting. At this time new items are added and old ones are dealt with from the top down. There is a running interaction with the events as they flow past. If a particular action item is never resolved, sometimes it can just be taken off the list. Things have a way of working themselves out in time!

Another form of agenda is one which carries three columns to the right of the list of agenda items. These columns are labeled "Information," "Discussion," and "Decision." An X is placed in one or more of the appropriate columns. For example, if an item is only to be presented at this meeting (and not discussed until the next meeting), an X would appear under "Information." If the item was to be both laid out and discussed, there would be an X under two columns. If it was hoped that you could both discuss it and reach a decision, the "Decision" column would also be checked. These X's in the three columns indicate the expectations of the meeting. This allows the person who is leading the meeting to maintain some control. Too often, after someone has given us a presentation, people immediately move into a problem-solving phase when actually they are not yet ready for that.

Another useful way of keeping an agenda creative and active is to list the approximate time when an item will be discussed to the right or the left of the agenda item. At the beginning of the meeting, if it is appropriate, the leader can ask for agreement that the time allowed is indeed realistic. Having received this agreement, he can use the schedule to control the flow of discussion. Many times it is more useful to leave an item unresolved and move on to the next item of business. As long as people are assured that the unresolved items will reappear on the next agenda, they will usually feel comfortable with this procedure.

A dear friend of ours is the chairperson of the missions committee in a large church. When she is faced with an apparent inability to move towards decision on an agenda item, she interrupts and suggests that two or three people pray about the particular item. If, during the course of the prayer time, she senses that resolution will still not be obtained, she moves on to the next agenda item. Her committee permits her to do this because its members know from experience that she will place this matter on the agenda for a subsequent meeting. Their experience also shows that the Holy Spirit seems to use this method to get the business accomplished!

Minutes.   These are probably the most abused and misused part of any meeting. How much the minutes need to recount all the details of the meeting is generally dependent upon the time between meetings on the same subject and whether such a meeting is ever going to be held again. For example, the yearly meeting of a board of directors might require very detailed minutes, while a weekly meeting of the education committee might require only limited ones.

You can also use as "minutes" the action items that were discussed above as "agenda." You can only make minutes from action items which have the responsible person(s) noted in the column to the right of the item. Probably these action items should be the first point of discussion at the next meeting.

Where Do Meetings Fit in Your Organization?

It is useful to analyze the different types of meetings that you are holding, remembering that the purpose of meetings is to inform members, discuss and solve problems, or reach decisions. Meetings have the side benefit of keeping people informed and in this sense can be great motivators. Recent studies have shown that the number-one reason for job satisfaction is the feeling of "being in on what's going on." This means that if you can use the meeting effectively to inform people, you can help them with their sense of belongingness.

Try to have all the meetings that you need, but try to make sure that you are allowing the right amount of time. For ongoing meetings, it is useful to cut them down to a shorter time period, whereas special meetings that are called for a specific purpose may need more time than is allotted. The reason for this is that people come to ongoing meetings with a great deal of information and history. On the other hand, when we call a meeting on a special subject, we need to allow enough time for people to become acclimated and get all of the background information that they need.

Evaluating Meetings

Just as any organizational task needs evaluation, so do meetings. There are a number of ways of doing this. We have heard of a technique in which one person is called a "fair communicator." It is this person's task to insure that people have an opportunity to be heard during the meeting and that accurate communication is taking place. Similarly, a person can be used as an evaluator of the meeting (or to lead the group through such an evaluation). By setting aside ten minutes at the end of any meeting and then asking the group to evaluate its own performance—as to leadership and participation—you may be surprised at how open people may become in assessing what is going on.

One really stimulating way to evaluate your performance as a leader, as well as the performances of other participants, is to use a closed-circuit videotape machine. Make a tape of the entire meeting. A review of the tape by the group will reveal all kinds of things!

Organizations are all about people coming together to perform a task outside of themselves. What meetings are about is helping those people discuss how they can more effectively accomplish their task. They are worth all the attention we can give them.

In Figure 21 we have reproduced a "meeting planner" which you might find a useful tool. Notice that the planner starts at the point at which every meeting should start: the *purpose*. Provision is made for both the short-term and long-range purpose. The next step should be the *procedure* that one is going to follow in carrying out the meeting. What kinds of methods are going to be employed? What kinds of tools will be necessary? At this point one can decide on *people*—those who will do the presenting, and those who will participate.

With this data in hand, it is now time to plan the program, including the schedule and facility. Don't forget about a *progress* report. After you have used this form to lay out your meeting, go back later and evaluate, including a decision about what to do "next time."

A great deal of an organization's life is dependent upon the effectiveness of the times when different

MEETING PLANNER

Date _____

MARC MANAGEMENT SERIES
Missions Advanced Research & Communication Center
919 West Huntington Drive
Monrovia, California 91016

PURPOSE

Short Term

Long Range

PROCEDURE

Methods

Tools

PEOPLE

Presenting

Participating

PROGRAM

Schedule

Facility

PROGRESS

Evaluation

Next Time . . .

Figure 21

members of the organization are together in a purposeful way. The manager who devotes tender loving care to the use of these meetings—recognizing that they take up a considerable amount of valuable time—will be much more effective than the manager who has a laissez-faire attitude about this tool.

Further Reading

Effective Committees and Groups in the Church by Ernest and Nancy Bormann is written as a layman's text from a rich background in the behavioral sciences.

Achieving Objectives in Meetings by Richard Cavalier is one of those "everything you always wanted to know about meetings, but were afraid you couldn't digest" books. But if you're involved in any kind of meeting, setting up meetings or conferences, trying to run a good meeting (large or small), this is a good book and worth its price.

Creative Management by Norman Maier and John Hayes classifies meetings by purpose and identifies the three basic kinds of meetings.

17

The Planning Conference

Whatever you do, do your work heartily, as for the Lord rather than for men.

Colossians 3:23

Planning is difficult to do in short bursts. It takes time, a commodity which is in continual short supply. "The tyranny of the urgent" is the enemy of planning. Just about the time we sit down together to figure out where to go next, our secretary announces a newly discovered brushfire which demands immediate attention. Good planning requires extended periods of quality time, the right mix of people, a facilitating environment, and adequate preparation. Good planning is a *result* of good planning!

We have identified the planning conference as a key element in building the organizational life cycle. By this we mean a conference which is isolated from the interruptions of everyday stress, purposely constructed to produce the desired result, and planned far enough in advance so that all needed participants can be available and adequately prepared.

How Often Is a Planning Conference Needed?

This is another way of asking, "How often should one plan?" Planning should be a continuous process. When we sit down at the end of the day or early in the morning to scratch out a "things to do" list, we are doing daily planning. When we put an hour aside on Mondays with members of our staff to talk about the week ahead, we are doing weekly planning. Many Christian organizations and local churches find that a monthly planning meeting with the entire professional staff is a good way to keep the house in order. However, in terms of setting new goals and deciding how we are going to reach them, we need to consider quarterly, biannual, or annual times together for the appropriate staff. This is what we mean by a planning conference.

What Is the Goal?

Most people assume that the goal of a planning conference is to plan. However, a better way of saying it is that the aim is to discover how to reach goals through plans. Therefore, it is necessary to include as early as possible on the agenda a definition of the goals—measurable, time-line statements of faith—that we expect to reach.

But a planning conference can have some other goals, not the least of which is team building. As we mentioned in the chapter on meetings, we need to set apart group members so that they learn to work together and know each other over an extended period of time. As they work together setting goals, making plans, and working to bring these goals into reality, they learn to appreciate each other's strong points and to work around each other's weaknesses. They have an opportunity to experience each other as individual people.

Another goal of the conference may be training. How you set up the conference and how you hold it will say a great deal in itself and will become a model that will help others to lead their own group's planning. The best way to learn to plan is to be part of an effective planning meeting.

What Is on the Agenda?

This answer should flow out of the goals that you have set for the conference. There will be announced goals and unannounced goals. Some of the latter would include how you want people to feel as a result of the conference and what modeling and training you want to do.

How you begin will do much to set the climate for the hours that follow. Take into account the total amount of time you have, how far afield you are willing to let people stray in their discussions, what kinds of finality you are hoping for in the "product" you would like to have at the end of the conference. If the goals you are working on are only roughly defined, clarify what needs to be an early item on the agenda. We will discuss evaluating goals below.

Make sure that the people at the conference have all the information they need to formulate the goals. This may be information brought with them, or it may be in the form of presentations needed for a common base of information. You may also need copies of annual reports, department or staff reports, data about the area in which you are working, and resources in the form of specialists or consultants.

Schedule time for a periodic change of pace. This may take the form of exercise, just plain relaxing, or going about the same problem in a different way. Remember, for most of us work can be really fun—except when we have too much of the same thing!

Somewhere on the agenda there should be a time of summarizing and drawing conclusions. When you leave, make sure that everyone understands his or her responsibilities and assignments. If you are going to use a planning system which is new to some of your staff (such as PERT, Gantt Charts, and so on), make sure that you have adequate training to give suitable instruction in its use.

This is a good opportunity to do some team building by having people work on sample planning problems and then try to analyze some of the difficulties of the system. This should be done before the actual planning conference. It will help to separate the process from the content.

Where Should You Hold a Conference?

Try to find a place that is sufficiently isolated from your headquarters, so that it will be "impossible" for you to be interrupted. It should be far enough away to make it difficult for people to return to their offices or homes, but not so distant that it would require too much travel time. Perhaps there is a retreat site an hour's drive away, or another church organization that is willing to lend you its facilities.

Make sure that the conference site is comfortable and that there are facilities for exercise breaks and other forms of relaxation. Have all the needed planning tools available: easels, equipment for projection, photo reproduction, dictating, and transcription—and anything else that you might use. Prepare a checklist ahead of time and make sure that in your negotiations for the facility you are clear as to what will be provided and what you will bring.

Who Should Come?

This can be a very sensitive question. It is even more difficult if you are going to move a number of people from the office. Their absence is going to be noticed, and people will draw their own conclusions about those who are invited. If at all possible, you should announce your reasons for choosing those you do. Obviously, you can work faster with a smaller number of people, but sometimes "the longer way around will be the shorter way home." The more people who are party to the planning, the more is the likelihood that you will get a good acceptance of the plans when an attempt is made to convert them to work.

You may want to differentiate between those who are going as the planning team and those who are resource people. There may be specialists who come in just to make presentations or to act as advisors. Make sure that the ground rules are well established, so that you avoid embarrassment.

Plan the Conference Carefully

Lay out a schedule of the events that must take place prior to the conference: people to be notified, material to be gathered, prior work to be accomplished. Build a checklist: facilities, equipment, visual and/or training aids, transportation arrangements, meals, and so on.

Put someone in charge of the *project* of holding the conference. The person need not necessarily be the leader, and this can be good training for the younger manager.

Understand the communication media that you will use. There is a difference between process and content. How people feel about the planning *process*, how they communicate with each other, and how they perceive the acceptance of their ideas will all have a direct bearing on an ultimate goal—which is usually expressed as *content*.

Review and rehearse. If you are taking ten people away for two days, you are utilizing a good many work hours. If you take an entire congregation away for a day, this is a big investment too. Get it all down right before you begin.

Evaluate as you proceed and also when you have finished. Usually an evaluation meeting halfway through will help the conference leaders discover which goals are not being met. Of course, if you are going to do a better job next time (and you should), you had better find out what was good and bad about this conference.

The Planning Conference As an Event

Some organizations, especially local churches, have discovered that the planning conference can be used as an all-organization event. The idea is to gather ideas from as many people as possible, with an eye toward having each person feel a part of the total process, sharing the goals and plans which may result. At first this may seem like an undertaking which could lead to nothing but chaos. Indeed, if chaos is to be avoided, such a conference will have to be well planned and well managed. Those doing the planning must have a good understanding about the participants and what process they must go through in order to come to useful conclusions.

The key to a successful conference is to spend a good deal of time in gathering data and sharing ideas. Here is where you can put to work what we have discussed on group planning techniques. By dividing into small subgroups which then brainstorm around different topics or goals, a way can be found to have each individual make a contribution. This must be more than just an exercise! Plan on ways of gathering information from the groups, synthesizing it, and then putting the groups back to work on higher priority items. Usually the best results are obtained if the group process is used to sort through perceived needs and desired goals. These needs and goals can then be prioritized, using the ABC Technique, and can in themselves become an overall statement against which detailed plans can be made.

Many times such conferences, particularly where volunteer organizations such as local churches are involved, can be conducted as a two-step process. The first session is used to gather ideas or to evaluate ideas that have already been gathered, while the second session is used to put groups to work in doing specific planning. In this case it is helpful to pretrain group leaders.

A Working Example

At the end of this chapter, we have reproduced a goal-evaluation form that was developed by one church. Before the planning conference, suggestions for goals had been gathered from various committees and individuals and a list compiled. About fifty goals were viewed by the planning team as being most important to the congregation. About a hundred and fifty people came to the planning conference, which was an all-day affair held in the offices of a large downtown corporation. The people were divided into groups of ten, and each group was given a number of suggested goals to evaluate against the items shown in Figure 22. The reporting form shown in Figure 23 was then used to report back to the entire group.

The entire morning was given over to evaluating the goals as they were seen by each group, which was then (after a lunch break) assigned the task of planning for the goal which it decided had the highest priority. Group leaders had previously been trained in the Slip and PERT methods. The Slip Technique was used to gather ideas as to how to reach the goal, and a PERT diagram was developed. At the end of the conference day, each group was given five minutes to "walk the audience through" the plan that it had developed.

The results of this planning day were highly profitable. A number of goal owners identified themselves as being particularly excited about some of the things they were planning. As a result, these individuals played a major role in establishing a help-line telephone ministry, in setting up a fellowship program for senior citizens

within the church, and in obtaining a business administrator for the church.

Further Reading

Achieving Objectives in Meetings by Richard Cavalier
(see reading list for chapter 16).

Figure 22
LAKE AVENUE CONGREGATIONAL CHURCH

EVALUATION

	Possible Maximum Rating	Your Rating

Project Name _____Number ____

I. Future Goals Evaluation

1. This project will build up the Body of Christ:
   a. At Lake Avenue Church. Who? _____   5
   b. In the San Gabriel Valley. Who? _____   5
   c. Beyond the San Gabriel Valley. Where? __   5

2. Number one will be accomplished by:
   a. More people praying   10
   b. God being more truly worshipped   10
   c. The existence of deeper Christian fellowship   10
   d. A better, broader interaction with God's Word   10
   e. More people finding a larger part of their lives given over (in *their* view) to God's service   15
   f. A fellowship of Christians honestly and actively seeking God's will   15

3. This project will give people a clear understanding of the Person of Jesus Christ (and therefore an opportunity to accept or reject Him) by:
   a. Verbal communication   5
   b. Written communication   5
   c. Audio-visual communication   10
   d. By demonstrating the power of Jesus Christ in the lives of His people   10

4. These means will lead people to decide for Jesus Christ because the means:
   a. Meet their needs   5
   b. Fit their cultural and social situations   5
   c. Have meaning for the total life situation of those being reached   10

5. This will be done in a manner that communicates:
   a. Once   5
   b. More than once   10
   c. Over a period of months   15
   d. Continually   20

6. This project will be:
   a. Similar to other projects we have undertaken   10
   b. New to many people   5
   c. Viewed by the church as new and dynamic   10
   d. Seen by the community as an exciting demonstration of Christian boldness   10

Future Goals Evaluation   220

Figure 22 (continued)
LAKE AVENUE CONGREGATIONAL CHURCH

	Possible Maximum Rating	Your Rating
EVALUATION		
Project Name _____Number ____		

II. Organization Evaluation

1. Who is responsible?
   a. This project logically falls under the jurisdiction of one of the existing boards: Deacons _____ Trustees _____ Other _____. — 20
   b. It appears to come under the jurisdiction of more than one board: _____ — 5
   c. We are unable to see how it fits under any one board — −5
   d. It could be carried out under the guidance of an existing committee — 10
   e. Would require a new board committee — −5
   f. Would require an independent committee — −10
   g. Could be managed by an individual reporting to an existing board _____ — 20

2. Who is leading? The needed leadership:
   a. Is available, for example _____ — 20
   b. Can be trained — 10
   c. Does not appear to be available at Lake Avenue — −10

3. Who is doing the work? The people who would be needed for this project are:
   a. Permanent staff — −10
   b. New staff — −20
   c. Church members — 20
   d. Non-church members — 10
   e. Available and motivated, e.g. _____ — 20
   f. Available, must be motivated — 10
   g. Available, must be trained — 5
   h. Perhaps not available — −10

4. This is being done by:
   a. No one else we know of — 20
   b. Within the church by _____ — 10
   c. Outside the church by _____ — −10

Organization Evaluation   100

Figure 22 (continued)
LAKE AVENUE CONGREGATIONAL CHURCH

EVALUATION	Possible Maximum Rating	Your Rating
Project Name _____Number ____		
III. People Evaluation		
1. This project will help:		
a. Church members	5	
b. New church members	5	
c. Staff	5	
d. People outside the church	10	
2. It will help them:		
a. Spiritually	10	
b. Socially	5	
c. Emotionally	5	
d. Materially	5	
e. Educationally	5	
People Evaluation	55	
IV. Present Situation Evaluation		
1. This project has been		
a. Never attempted or considered	5	
b. Tried ineffectively	−5	
c. Carried out effectively. By whom? _____	10	
2. Most of the people of Lake Avenue Church think that this is or will be a worthwhile project.	20	
3. The staff is probably ready to accept it.	20	
4. The boards are probably ready to accept it.	20	
5. Financially, it:		
a. Would probably fit into our present budget	20	
b. Would require minor outlay over our present budget	10	
c. Would require a major one-time outlay over the present budget	−10	
d. Would require a continuing outlay over present expenditures	−10	
6 Facilities:		
a. Existing facilities O.K.	20	
b. With new building, facilities O.K.	10	
c. Probably have to go outside for facilities	5	
d. Need expenditure for facilities	−10	
7. Schedule:		
a. Needs a long-term planning phase	5	
b. Requires a short-term planning phase	10	
c. Probably ready to implement as soon as accepted by boards and/or congregation	20	
Present Situation Evaluation	140	
PROJECT NAME _____TOTAL	515	

Figure 23
LAKE AVENUE CONGREGATIONAL CHURCH
PLANNING CONFERENCE   GOD'S WAY FOR OUR DAY

Fill in the most appropriate word or phrase from your evaluation sheet. See referenced paragraph number.

PROJECT EVALUATION REPORT

We have evaluated the project called _____
We have further defined the purpose and goal of the project as follows: _____
_____

In relating this project to our ten-year suggested goal, we think that it will communicate the Person of Jesus Christ (1) _____
(2) _____

I. Future Goals Evaluation

It will build up the Body of Christ (I. 1) _____
This project will be (I.6) _____
   in that _____
If this project is carried out, the Body of Christ will be built up by (I.2): ___
_____

Our overall rating of this project in terms of the future goal is _____
out of a possible _____.

II. Organization Evaluation

In terms of organization we believe that the jurisdiction of this project logically rests with (II.1) _____
It is our opinion that leadership is (II.2) _____
   and that the personnel needed are (II.3) _____
That this is being done by (II.4) _____
Our overall organization rating is _____ out of a possible
_____.

III People Evaluation

In terms of the people whom the project would serve, we think it will help
(III.1) _____
It will help them (III.2) _____
We rate this phase _____ out of a possible _____.

IV Present Situation Evaluation

As we look at the present church situation we believe that a project such as
this has (IV.1) _____
It appears that a significant number of people (IV.2) _____ this is a
meaningful project. The staff (IV.3) _____ ready to accept it. The
boards are (IV.4) _____ ready to accept it.
Financially, it is our estimate that (IV.5) _____
Facilities (IV. 6) _____
This project requires (IV.7) _____ planning.
Our present situation evaluation resulted in a score of _____ out of a possible _____, resulting in a total evaluation of _____ out of a possible _____.
On this basis we would give this project a score of (1–10) _____.
In addition, our study group _____
_____

Bibliography

Argyris, Chris. *Increasing Leadership Effectiveness.* New York: Wiley, 1976.

Bennis, Warren. *Organization Development: Its Nature, Origin and Prospects.* Reading, Massachusetts: Addison-Wesley, 1969.

Bormann, Ernest and Nancy. *Effective Committees and Groups in the Church.* Minneapolis: Augsburg Publishing House, 1973.

Cavalier, Richard. *Achieving Objectives in Meetings.* New York: Corporate Movement, 1973.

Churchman, C. West. *The Systems Approach.* New York: Della Publishing, 1969.

Crosby, Philip B. *The Art of Getting Your Own Sweet Way.* New York: McGraw-Hill, 1972.

Dale, Ernest. *Organization.* New York: American Management Association, 1967.

Dayton, Edward R. *God's Purpose and Man's Plans.* Monrovia, California: MARC, 1971.

_____. *Tools for Time Management.* Grand Rapids, Michigan: Zondervan, 1974.

Dayton, Edward R., and Engstrom, Ted W. *Strategy for Living.* Glendale, California: Regal Books, 1976.

Drucker, Peter F. *The Effective Executive.* New York: Harper & Row, 1967.

Engel, James F. *How Can I Get Them to Listen?* Grand Rapids, Michigan: Zondervan, 1977.

Engel, James F., and Norton, W. Wilbert. *What's Gone Wrong with the Harvest?* Grand Rapids, Michigan: Zondervan, 1975.

Engstrom, Ted W. *The Making of a Christian Leader.* Grand Rapids, Michigan: Zondervan, 1976.

Engstrom, Ted W., and Dayton, Edward R. *The Art of Management for Christian Leaders.* Waco, Texas: Word, 1976.

Engstrom, Ted W., and MacKenzie, Alex. *Managing Your Time.* Grand Rapids, Michigan: Zondervan, 1968.

Ewing, David W. *The Human Side of Planning.* New York: Macmillan, 1969.

Gangel, Kenneth. *Competent to Lead: A Guide to Management in Christian Organizations.* Chicago: Moody Press, 1974.

Getz, Gene A. *Sharpening the Focus of the Church.* Chicago: Moody Press, 1974.

Hendrix, Olan. *Management for the Christian Worker.* Santa Barbara, California: Quill Publications, 1976.

Hughes, Charles L. *Goal Setting: Key to Organizational Effectiveness.* New York: American Management Association, 1965.

Janis, Irving. *Victims of Groupthink.* Boston and New York: Houghton Mifflin, 1973.

Johnson, David W., and Johnson, Frank P. *Joining Together: Group Theory and Group Skills.* Englewood Cliffs, New Jersey: Prentice-Hall, 1975.

Kelley, Dean M. *Why Conservative Churches Are Growing.* New York: Harper & Row, 1972.

Kepner, Charles H., and Tregoe, B. B. *The Rational Manager: A Systematic Approach to Problem Solving and Decision Making.* New York: McGraw-Hill, 1965.

Kiev, Ari. *A Strategy for Daily Living.* New York: The Free Press, 1973.

Lakein, Alan. *How to Get Control of Your Time and Your Life.* New York: Wyden, 1973.

Luft, Joseph. *Group Processes: An Introduction to*

Group Dynamics. Palo Alto, California: Mayfield Publishing, 1970.

McConkey, Dale D. *Goal Setting: A Guide to Achieving the Church's Mission.* Minneapolis: Augsburg, 1978.

MacKenzie, Alex. *The Time Trap: Managing Your Way Out.* New York: American Management Association, 1972.

Mager, Robert F. *Goal Analysis.* Belmont, California: Fearon, 1972.

Mager, Robert F., and Pipe, Peter. *Analyzing Performance Problems; or, You Really Oughta Wanna.* Belmont, California: Fearon, 1970.

Maier, Norman, and Hayes, John. *Creative Management.* New York: Wiley, 1962.

Ortlund, Raymond C. *Lord, Make My Life a Miracle.* Glendale, California: Regal Books, 1974.

Reddin, W. J. *Effective Management by Objectives: The 3-D Method of MBO.* New York: McGraw-Hill, 1971.

Richards, Lawrence. *A Theology of Christian Education.* Grand Rapids, Michigan: Zondervan, 1975.

Schaller, Lyle E. *Parish Planning.* Nashville: Abingdon, 1971.

––––––. *The Change Agent: The Strategy of Innovative Leadership.* Nashville: Abingdon, 1972.

––––––. *The Decision-Makers.* Nashville: Abingdon, 1974.

Simon, Sidney B. *Meeting Yourself Halfway.* Niles, Illinois: Argus Communications.

Index

ABC Technique, 144, 182, 226
  described, 204, 205, 206
Accountability, 65
Achieving, 48
Action, 43, 150
  implementing plan, 103
Administration, church, 68
Agendas, 214, 223
  creative, 215
Alinsky, Sol, 114
Alternatives, 89
Analysis, situation, 118
Anatomy (organization), 26
Annual report, 127
Approach, overall, 133
Argyris, Chris, 152
Assumptions, 67, 73, 86
  about Christian organizations, 33
  failure to state, 88
  list of, 87
  shared, 174
Augustine, Saint, 161
Authority, 26
  lines of, 21

Bennis, Warren, 30
Biblical priorities, 69
Bormann, Ernest, and Nancy, 220
Brainstorming, 176
Budget, 102
  annual, 128
  planning by extrapolation, 128

Calvin, John, 161
Cavalier, Richard, 220, 228
Chalkboard Technique, 177, 180
Change agent, 113, 132
Checklist
  goals, 229
  organizational life cycle, 117

Christian organization
  assumptions, 33
  defined, 31
  differences, 32
  purpose, 7
Church, 70
  growth, 40
  local, 39, 83, 90, 128, 149
  local PERT, 199
  not economic organization, 162
  planning, 161
Commitment, levels of, 71
Commitments, 119
  of the organization, 28
Committee, planning, 130
Committees, 174
  effective, 220
Communication, 25, 27
  lines of, 21
  through planning, 83
Communicator, fair, 217
Complexity levels, 90
Compromise, 147
Concepts, putting to work, 110
Conference, planning, 142
Conflict management, 147
Conflicts, resolving, 146
Correction, 43, 112
Courage and decisions, 89
Creative tension, 28
Crosby, Philip B., 121
Cycle, organizational. See Organizational cycle

Dale, Ernest, 30
Data gathering, 120, 175
  techniques, 181
Decision, 86
  making, 152
  risk taking, 85
Delegation, 67
Delphi Technique, 181

De-motivators, 125
Detail, tight to, 125
Direction, sense of, 56
Displaying
 ideas, 186
 plans, 191
Drucker, Peter F., 17

Edison, Thomas, 102
Effectiveness, 57
 leadership, 152
Eisenhower, Dwight D., 203
Enablers, 143, 206
Engel, James F., 139
Enthusiasm, goals promote, 56
Environment, enabling, 22
Estimating, 201
Evaluate, 150
Evaluation, 44, 57, 82, 112, 207
 idea, 184
 report form, 232
Events, important, 143
Ewing, David, 79, 82, 84, 93, 132
Expectations, developing realis-
 tic, 89
Experience, 131
 known, 99, 106

Facilitators, 143, 206
Failure, 55, 80
Faith, statement of, 86
Fear
 of failure, 55
 of goals, 55
Feedback, 139, 145
Finances, availability of, 88
Foster, Gerald P., 157
Functions, overlapping, 45
Future, 85, 162

Gangel, Kenneth, 40
Gantt Chart, 182, 187, 194
Getz, Gene, 17, 40
Goal
 defined, 52, 53
 future event, 54
 image of the future, 53
 owners, 59, 64, 193
 potential, 145
 planning conference, 222
 setting, 41
  a process, 62

Goal (cont.)
 statement of faith, 53
Goals, 111, 131, 134
 annual, local church, 92
 arranged by purposes, 141
 assumptions about, 67
 broad, 87
 developed from within, 34
 establishment of, 123
 evaluating checklist, 229
 evaluation, 143, 229, 230, 231
 fear of, 55
 for organizational effectiveness, 29
 future, 120
 fuzzy, 61, 68
 good and bad, 67
 guidelines for setting, 65
 in time, 60
 operational, 63
 poorly written, 62
 power of, 51
 prioritizing, 144
 relationships, 58
 statements of faith, 55, 62, 67
 steps for, 140
 too high, 59
 unrealistic, 63
 unreconcilable, 39
 well written, 62
God's will, 116
God's work, 77
Group dynamics, 152
Group planning, 175
Group process, 206
Growth cycle, organizational, 41
Guide for problem solvers, 105
Guidelines, 89
Guinness, Os, 169

Hall, Edward T., 163
Hayes, John, 212, 220
Hendrix, Olan, 17
Herzberg, Frederick, 125
History, 118
 impact on organization, 27
Holy Spirit, 34, 48, 123, 134, 216
 ability of, 79
 trying to do the work of, 55
Hughes, Charles L., 68
Hygienic elements, 125

Idea
  evaluation, 184
  integration, 185
Ideas
  arranged by category, 138
  displaying of, 186
  ordering and evaluating, 182
  samples of, 136
Inflation, 88
Information gathering, 135
Integration, idea, 185

Janis, Irving L., 174
Johnson, David W., 152, 190
Johnson, Frank P., 152, 190

Kelley, Dean, 24
Kennedy, John, 160
Kepner, Charles H., 108
Kiev, Ari, 153

Lakein, Alan, 153
Leadership styles, 35
Leas, Speed, 151, 154
List, 192
  of assumptions, 88
  project, 186, 193
  random, 186
Living, daily, 153
Local church, 142
Logic diagram, 187
Long-range planning, steps, 86
Luft, Joseph, 152

Machiavelli, Prince, 114
Mackenzie, Alec, 17, 153
Mager, Robert F., 54, 108
Maier, Norman, 212, 220
Malony, H. Newton, 162, 169
Management by Objective
    (MBO), 57, 126, 151
Management
  for mission, 63
  time, 152
MBO. *See* Management by Ob-
    jective
McKonkey, Dale B., 68
Meeting planner, 219
Meetings, 208
  church, 210
  elements of good, 213
  evaluating, 217

Meetings (cont.)
  in the organization, 216
  kinds of, 211
  minutes, 216
Milestones, 89
Money
  cost of raising, 90
  raising, 129
Motivation, 125, 145
  reasons for, 126

Needs, felt, 88
Newsprint Technique, 177, 180
Nurture, Christian, 138

Objectives of ministry, 130
Opposition, loyal, 174
Organization
  anatomy of, 19, 26
  charts, 113
  commitments, 28
  goals, 28
  purpose of, 86, 124, 135
  volunteer, 38
Organizational cycle, 42, 111
  advantages of, 113
  entry points, 126
Organizational
  development, 30
  life cycle, checklist, 117
  orbit, 115
Organizations
  ad hoc, 20
  boundaries, 24
  causes for failure, 47
  complexity, 21
  defined, 20, 111
  in the larger system, 21
  level and breadth, 37
  not-for-profit, 36
  priorities of, 72
  profit, 37
  seen in tension, 27
Organizing, 43
Ortlund, Raymond C., 75
Output, emphasis on, 58
Outreach, 138

Para-church, 32
Paradox, 73

Patience, 128
People, motivated, 24
Person-hours, 202
PERT, 177, 187, 196
  local church, 199
  Technique, 144
Pipe, Peter, 108
Planning, 42, 112
  ahead, 57
  and problem solving, 78, 165
  annual, 82
  as arrow, 80, 91
  as future history, 80
  as process, 81, 151
  as way of life, 77
  church, 82
  committee, 130
    purposes of, 130, 131
  conference, 221
    report form, 232
  effective, 77
  elements of, 79
  focus, 92
  in the church, 161
  inadequate, 47
  long-range, 140
    defined, 85
  monthly meeting, 222
  parish, 84
  preparation for, 142
  process, 124
  putting to work, 91
  retreat, 142
  techniques, group, 173
  to do God's work, 77
  tools, 191
Plans, displaying, 191
Posteriorities, 74
Prayer groups, 175
Priority
  Christian levels of, 69
  considerations, 203, 204
  highest, 74
Priorities, 111
  biblical, 69
  defined, 69
  functional, 74
  recognizing, 73
  setting, 202
  too many, 47

Problem
  deviation from goal, 97
  understanding the, 105
Problem solvers' guide, 105
Problem solving, 95
  basic steps, 96
  logical elements, 7, 98
  versus planning, 96
Process, repetitive, 44
Processes, group, 152
Project evaluation report, 232
Purpose
  defined, 52
  organizational, 24
  statement of, 135
Purposes, 111
  given from God, 34
  in goal setting, 41
  need for, 25
  spiritualized, 53

Reddin, W. J., 151
Relationships
  complexity of, 21
  quality of, 70
Report, annual, 127
Research, 181
  defined, 100
Resources, 64, 102, 149
  adequate, 25
  defined, 25
  gathering, 103
Responsibility, assigning, 148
Results, 67
  using, 104
Retreat, planning, 142
Richards, Lawrence, 84
Risk taking, 86

Scenarios, 167, 168, 169
Schaller, Lyle, 84, 132, 152
Schedules, 149
Scheduling, 200
Seminar program, 197
Simon, Sidney P., 152
Situation analysis, 118, 134
Situation, present, 120
Skills, adequate, 25
Slip Technique, 144, 146, 177, 227
  adaptability of, 187

Slip Technique (cont.)
  advantages, 189
  cautions, 189
  idea arrangement, 183
  uses, 184
Sovereignty, God's 55
Spectrum, organizational, 36
Spinout, 115, 116
Staff, paid, 164
Statement of faith
  defined, 87
  official, 87
Statements of faith, 127
Strategy, overall, 100, 106
Structure, 25
Success, cause of failure, 48
Surveys, 139

Technique, ABC. *See* ABC
  Technique

Technique, Chalkboard. *See*
  Chalkboard Technique
Technique, PERT. *See* PERT
Technique, Slip. *See* Slip
  Technique
Thinking, traditional, 118
Time
  elapsed, 202
  estimates, 201
Tools, planning, 191
Tradition, 118
Training, 222
Tregoe, Benjamin B., 108

Values, 33
Vaux, Kenneth, 169
Volunteers, 72

Walking wounded, 39